Python for Beginners

A Visual Guide to Start Quickly

**Comes with
Support on :**

 GitHub

 Community

Follow Us on :

 Medium

 Linkedin

Basics>Strong;

How
to get the most out of this Book

Start with the Book

Dive into each chapter for a solid foundation. This book is your roadmap—each chapter builds on the last, so take it one step at a time. Its a very quick read and comes with practice projects so take the full advantage.

Follow Us on Medium for Fresh Insights

Stay inspired and informed by following us on Medium! We regularly post articles with extra tips, real-world examples, and thought-provoking discussions to deepen your understanding.
https://medium.com/
@basicsstrong

Practice with the Code on GitHub

Practice makes perfect! Our GitHub repo has all the code samples and solutions ready for you to explore, tweak, and play around with.
https://github.com/
basicsstrong

Join Our Community

Want to learn alongside others? For the **price of a pizza slice**, you can join our exclusive community. Here, you'll get:

- Webinars
- Answer of all your questions
- Mentoring sessions
- A space to connect with like-minded people on the same journey as you!

https://www.skool.com/
pythonlearningcommunity

THIS BOOK IS CRAFTED WITH A LOT OF

Hello, my name is

MOHIT SINGHAL

I am an Enterprise Architect with a 20+ year journey through the tech world. Fueled by curiosity and innovation, I'm here to explore, create, and share insights that make technology accessible and exciting.

CONNECT WITH US:

1. Mohit Singhal
linkedin.com/in/mohitsinghal-software-architect/

2. Meenal Bhansali
linkedin.com/in/meenal-bhansali/

3. Follow Basics Strong
linkedin.com/company/basics-strong

Hi! I am

MEENAL BHANSALI

a passionate developer and Architect with 8+ years of experience, committed to transforming ideas into reality through code and creative problem-solving.

Together with our dynamic creative team, we're thrilled to present this book. We're here not just to teach but to inspire, helping you break down complex topics with ease and clarity.

THIS BOOK IS CRAFTED WITH A LOT OF

Hello, my name is
MOHIT SINGHAL

I am an Enterprise Architect with a 20+ year journey through the tech world. Fueled by curiosity and innovation, I'm here to explore, create, and share insights that make technology accessible and exciting.

CONNECT WITH US:

1. **Mohit Singhal**
linkedin.com/in/mohitsinghal-software-architect/

2. **Meenal Bhansali**
linkedin.com/in/meenal-bhansali/

3. **Follow Basics Strong**
linkedin.com/company/basics-strong

Hi! I am
MEENAL BHANSALI

a passionate developer and Architect with 8+ years of experience, committed to transforming ideas into reality through code and creative problem-solving.

Together with our dynamic creative team, we're thrilled to present this book. We're here not just to teach but to inspire, helping you break down complex topics with ease and clarity.

How
to get the most out of this Book

Start with the Book

Dive into each chapter for a solid foundation. This book is your roadmap—each chapter builds on the last, so take it one step at a time. Its a very quick read and comes with practice projects so take the full advantage.

Practice with the Code on GitHub

Practice makes perfect! Our GitHub repo has all the code samples and solutions ready for you to explore, tweak, and play around with.
https://github.com/ basicsstrong

Follow Us on Medium for Fresh Insights

Stay inspired and informed by following us on Medium! We regularly post articles with extra tips, real-world examples, and thought-provoking discussions to deepen your understanding.
https://medium.com/ @basicsstrong

Join Our Community

Want to learn alongside others? For the **price of a pizza slice**, you can join our exclusive community. Here, you'll get:

- Webinars
- Answer of all your questions
- Mentoring sessions
- A space to connect with like-minded people on the same journey as you!

https://www.skool.com/ pythonlearningcommunity

Python ProgrammingCore Series

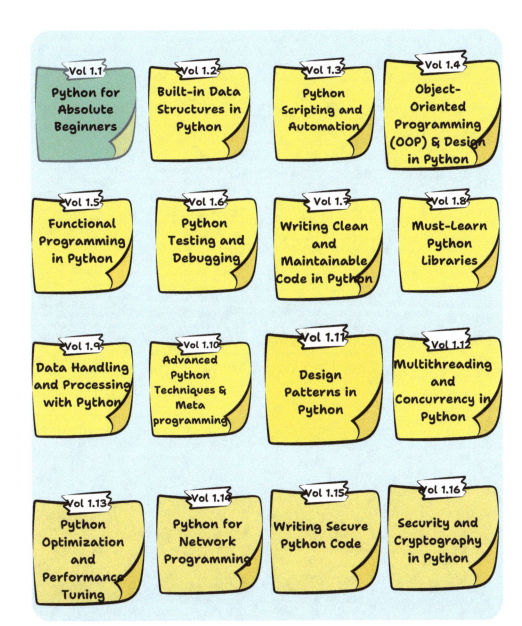

Table of Contents

115
Functions and Modules

- DEFINING FUNCTIONS
- PARAMETERS AND RETURN VALUES
- SCOPE AND LIFETIME OF VARIABLES
- BUILT-IN FUNCTIONS VS. USER-DEFINED FUNCTIONS
- IMPORTING AND USING MODULES

7

125
Data Structures

- LISTS: CREATING, ACCESSING, AND MODIFYING
- TUPLES AND IMMUTABLE SEQUENCES
- DICTIONARIES: KEY-VALUE PAIRS
- SETS AND SET OPERATIONS
- WORKING WITH DATA STRUCTURES

8

137
String Manipulation

- BASIC STRING OPERATIONS
- STRING METHODS AND FORMATTING
- F-STRINGS AND FORMAT()
- WORKING WITH MULTILINE STRINGS

9

148
Error and Exception Handling

- TYPES OF ERRORS IN PYTHON
- TRY, EXCEPT, ELSE, AND FINALLY
- RAISING EXCEPTIONS
- COMMON EXCEPTION TYPES

10

158
File Handling

- READING FROM AND WRITING TO FILES
- WORKING WITH DIFFERENT FILE MODES
- EXCEPTION HANDLING IN FILE OPERATIONS
- USING WITH FOR FILE MANAGEMENT

11

168
Object-Oriented Programming (OOP) Basics

- CLASSES AND OBJECTS
- ATTRIBUTES AND METHODS
- CONSTRUCTORS AND DESTRUCTORS
- INHERITANCE, ENCAPSULATION, AND POLYMORPHISM

12

180

Working with Libraries and Packages

- INSTALLING EXTERNAL LIBRARIES WITH PIP
- COMMONLY USED PYTHON LIBRARIES: MATH, RANDOM, DATETIME
- INTRODUCTION TO NUMPY FOR ARRAYS AND DATA ANALYSIS

13

14

191

Project: Building a Small Python Application

- DEFINING THE PROJECT SCOPE
- BUILDING THE APPLICATION STEP-BY-STEP
- TESTING AND DEBUGGING
- DOCUMENTING THE CODE

208

Next Steps in Python

15

- EXPLORING ADVANCED TOPICS IN PYTHON
- RESOURCES FOR FURTHER LEARNING
- OVERVIEW OF SPECIALIZED AREAS (E.G., WEB DEVELOPMENT, DATA SCIENCE)

Introduction to
PROGRAMMING

What are we going to learn?

1. What is Programming?
2. Programming Languages Overview
3. Basic Concepts in Programming
4. Understanding How Code is Executed
5. Getting into the Programmer's Mindset

Programming is the art of turning ideas into instructions for machines. It brings your creativity to life—automating tasks, solving problems, and building amazing experiences like apps and games. It's more than code; it's about thinking critically, breaking down problems, and creating smart solutions step by step

What is programming?

Programming is giving instructions to machine to get the tasks done.

So, how are these instructions given?

Do you directly ask the machine to perform your task?

Let's see!

Instructing a Human:

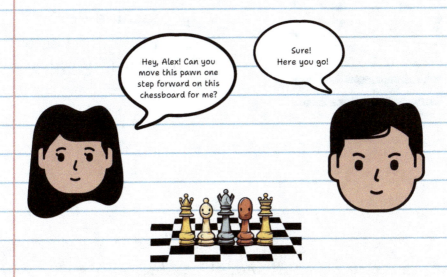

Can Machine work in same fashion?

Instructing a Machine:

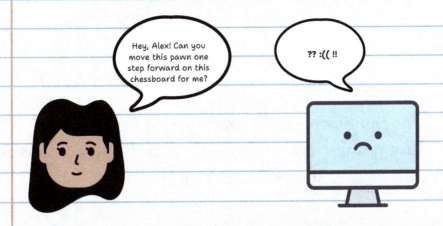

3

The machine doesn't understand if you simply speak to it in English.

(Unless there's some kind of AI conversion machine understands! like ChatGpt)
that translates English into a language the

machine understands!)

Machines can only understand instructions in a language that can be processed and converted into machine instructions.

```
def move_pawn(left, right, top, bottom) :
  left = left + 1;
```

If we convert this into human-readable instructions, it might look something like this:

1. **Function**: move_pawn
2. **Purpose**: Adjust the pawn's position by moving it one step to the left.
3. **How it works**:
   1. Take in the current position values for left, right, top, and bottom.
   2. Increase the left position by 1, moving the pawn one step to the right.

✦ This is exactly what programming is!

You don't have to fully understand this syntax right now. We'll spend time in upcoming lectures to go over the syntax and everything in detail. This is just to give you an idea of what programming looks like!

But why would we Even write code to
do such a simple task?

Let's understand this with the following points:

1. The tasks we perform can be complex and time-consuming. Computers can handle these complex tasks more efficiently if we code them correctly.

2. Tasks can be repetitive, whether simple or complex. These repetitive tasks need to be automated.

Everything you see nowadays—online shopping, internet banking, gaming on your phone or computer—is nothing but programs taking your inputs and responding with pre-set instructions (code 😊).

1.2 Programming languages overview

Programming Languages Overview

In this chapter, we'll dive into the world of programming languages and understand how they help us communicate with machines! Let's explore the basics and see why different types of languages exist and how they're used.

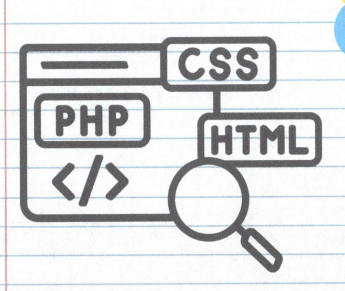

High-level vs. Low-level Languages

Imagine talking to a friend vs. talking to a machine directly! High-level and low-level languages are like these two different types of conversations.

High-level Languages

These are closer to human languages and easier for us to understand. High-level languages handle many complex details for us, allowing us to focus on solving problems without worrying about the machine's inner workings. Examples include **Python**, **JavaScript**, and **Ruby**.

Low-level Languages

These languages are closer to the machine's language. They're harder for humans to understand but give more control over the hardware. These include **Assembly** and **Machine Code**. They allow programmers to interact directly with the computer's memory and processor

Think of high-level languages as giving directions using landmarks ("Turn left at the big tree!") and low-level languages as giving GPS coordinates. Both get you to the same place, but one is simpler for us, while the other is precise for the machine!

Examples of Popular Languages and Their Uses

Let's look at some popular programming languages and where you might encounter them:

Python
Often known as the "beginner-friendly" language, Python is used everywhere from data science to web development to automation. Its simple syntax makes it a favorite for new programmers and experts alike.

JavaScript

The language of the web! JavaScript brings websites to life, making them interactive and dynamic. If you've ever clicked a button on a website that did something cool, JavaScript was likely behind it.

Java
Known for its "write once, run anywhere" capability, Java is widely used in Android apps, enterprise software, and large systems that need to be stable and reliable.

C++

A powerful language used in game development, systems programming, and applications requiring high performance. C++ gives programmers control over system resources, making it popular for resource-intensive tasks.

Ruby

Often used in web development, Ruby is known for its elegant syntax and is a favorite among developers who build web applications quickly. The popular framework **Ruby on Rails** is based on Ruby.

Fun Fact

Each language has its unique personality! Some are efficient and powerful, while others are fun and flexible. Choosing a language often depends on the task you want to accomplish.

Why Do We Need Different Languages?

Every language has its strengths and weaknesses, just like different tools in a toolbox. Some languages are better for building fast applications, while others are easier to learn and work with. The variety of languages allows programmers to choose the right tool for the job, whether they're building websites, analyzing data, or programming robots.

So, we learned about the difference between high-level and low-level languages and got introduced to some popular programming languages. Just like learning different languages can help us travel the world, learning different programming languages opens up new possibilities in the world of technology!

1.3 Basics concepts in programming

Basic Concepts in programming

Welcome to the core of programming! Here, we'll uncover some essential building blocks that will set you up for success in writing code. Think of this as learning the fundamentals of how to approach a problem, break it down, and map out your solution in a clear, logical way. Let's dive in!

Algorithms and Problem Solving

At the heart of programming is **problem-solving** and the way we solve problems with code is by creating **algorithms**. But what exactly is an algorithm?

What is an Algorithm?

An algorithm is simply a **step-by-step set of instructions** to solve a problem. Think of it as a recipe! Just like a recipe has specific steps to make a dish, an algorithm has steps to achieve a specific outcome in a program.

Problem-Solving with Algorithms

When you have a problem, the first step is to understand it fully and break it down into smaller parts. Then, you can write out an algorithm that provides a clear, logical path to the solution. This approach keeps you organized and helps avoid mistakes.

Example

Imagine you're writing an algorithm to make a peanut butter sandwich. The steps might look like this:

Get two slices of bread.

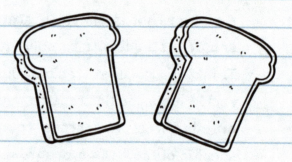

Spread peanut butter on one slice

Spread jelly on the other slice

Put the two slices together

This simple recipe is like an algorithm for making a sandwich!

Writing Pseudocode

Now that you understand the basics of an algorithm, let's look at **pseudocode.** Pseudocode is like a rough draft of your code — it's not in any specific programming language, but it's written in plain English

Why Use Pseudocode?

Pseudocode helps you map out your algorithm without worrying about syntax. It's a way to focus on the logic of your solution and make sure your steps are clear before you start coding.

How to Write Pseudocode

Start by writing each step of your solution in a clear, concise way. Don't worry about getting it perfect — the idea is to create an easy-to-follow outline.

Example of Pseudocode for Checking if a Number is Even:

```
START
 INPUT number
 IF number MOD 2 == 0 THEN
  PRINT "The number is even"
 ELSE
  PRINT "The number is odd"
 ENDIF
 END
```

This simple pseudocode gives a clear outline of what the program should do, without any complex syntax.

Flowcharts for Visualizing Program Logic

Another tool in your programming toolbox is the **flowchart**. Flowcharts are diagrams that visually represent the flow of your program's logic. They help you see the big picture and understand how different parts of your program connect.

Why Use Flowcharts?

Flowcharts are especially useful when you're working on a complex problem. They allow you to visualize the steps and decisions in your algorithm, making it easier to catch errors or identify improvements.

Flowchart Symbols

Flowcharts use different symbols to represent different types of actions:

- **Oval**: Start or End of the process
- **Rectangle**: A process or action
- **Diamond**: A decision point (like an "if" statement)
- **Arrow**: Shows the direction of flow

18

Example Flowchart:
Making a Decision to Buy Coffee

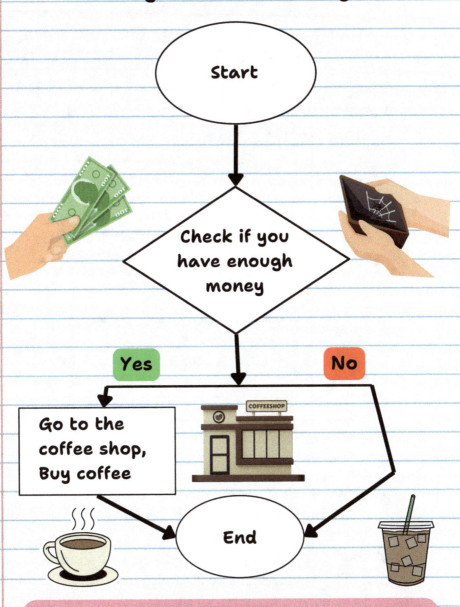

This simple flowchart shows the decision process for buying coffee and the different steps involved.

Why These Concepts Matter

Learning to structure your thoughts with algorithms, pseudocode, and flowcharts sets a strong foundation for programming. These tools are your roadmap to create well-thought-out solutions before you dive into writing code, making the coding process much smoother.

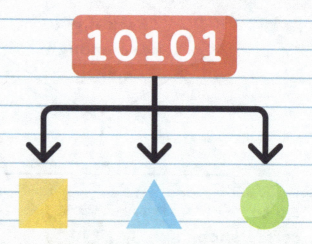

Summary

In this chapter, we explored the basics of problem-solving with algorithms, writing pseudocode to map out logic, and using flowcharts to visualize program flow. These concepts will help you approach any problem with a structured plan!

1.4 Undestanding How Code is executed

Understanding How Code is Executed

Now that we have a solid foundation in problem-solving and structuring ideas, let's explore what happens when we actually run our code. How does a machine understand our instructions? This chapter will guide you through the magic behind code execution and how different programming languages handle it.

1. Compilers vs. Interpreters

To understand how code is executed, we need to talk about compilers and interpreters. These are the tools that take our code and make it understandable for the machine.

<CODE/>

- **Compilers**

A compiler translates the entire code (or program) into machine language (binary code) in one go before the program is run. Once the code is compiled, it creates an executable file that can be run without further translation. This is common for languages like **C++** and **Java.**

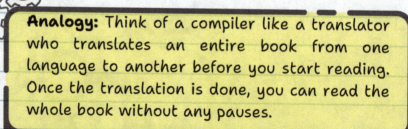

Analogy: Think of a compiler like a translator who translates an entire book from one language to another before you start reading. Once the translation is done, you can read the whole book without any pauses.

- ## Interpreters

An interpreter, on the other hand, translates the code line-by-line as the program runs. This means the code is executed directly, without creating a separate executable file. This is how **Python** works!

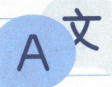

- **Analogy:** An interpreter is like a translator who translates each sentence as you read it. This allows you to read the book in real-time but might be a bit slower since each line has to be translated on the spot.

- **Speed and Flexibility**

Compilers are generally faster because the entire code is translated at once, while interpreters allow more flexibility, making it easier to test and debug code line-by-line.

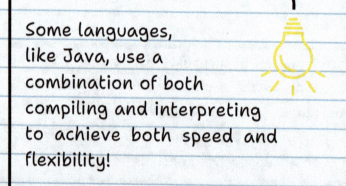

Some languages, like Java, use a combination of both compiling and interpreting to achieve both speed and flexibility!

DID YOU KNOW?

2. How Python Interprets Code

Python is an **interpreted language**, meaning it reads and executes code line-by-line. But there's a bit more happening under the hood!

- **Python's Interpreter**

When you write and run Python code, the Python interpreter does the heavy lifting.

Here's a simplified view of the process:

1. **Source Code:** You write your code in a Python file (.py).
2. **Compilation to Bytecode:** Python first compiles your code into an intermediate form called bytecode. This isn't machine code, but a low-level representation that's easier for the machine to work with.
3. **Execution by the Python Virtual Machine (PVM):** The bytecode is then executed by the Python Virtual Machine (PVM), which interprets it line-by-line and translates it into machine instructions that the computer can understand.

- ## Analogy

Imagine you have a recipe written in English (source code). Python translates it into a set of simple, easy-to-follow steps (bytecode). Then, the PVM acts as the chef, executing each step carefully in sequence to create the final dish (program output).

- ## Why Python is Slower but More Flexible

Python is called an interpreted language because the interpreter handles everything—even behind-the-scenes compilation! Unlike Java, Python compiles code into bytecode (not machine code) and then interprets it line-by-line with the Python Virtual Machine (PVM). This makes Python flexible and easy to use, but a bit slower—like a translator reading instructions step-by-step instead of speaking directly to the machine."
However, its flexibility and ease of use make it a favorite for many programmers, especially for tasks like web development, data analysis, and automation.

26

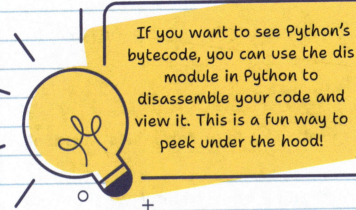

If you want to see Python's bytecode, you can use the dis module in Python to disassemble your code and view it. This is a fun way to peek under the hood!

Why Execution Matters?

Understanding how code is executed helps you write more efficient programs and troubleshoot issues more effectively. Knowing whether your language is compiled or interpreted also gives you insight into its strengths and limitations.

Summary

In this chapter, we explored how code is executed with the help of compilers and interpreters, and learned about Python's unique process of interpreting code through bytecode and the Python Virtual Machine. This foundational knowledge will make you a better programmer as you begin to dive deeper into coding!

1.4 Programmer's Mindset

Getting into the Programmer's Mindset

Programming isn't just about writing code —it's about how you think! To be a good programmer, you need to adopt a certain mindset that helps you tackle complex problems, stay persistent, and constantly improve. In this chapter, we'll look at the habits and ways of thinking that help programmers succeed.

1. Importance of Logic and Analytical Thinking

At the core of programming is **logic**. Logic is all about understanding cause and effect, making decisions, and thinking in a structured way.

- ### Why Logic is Key

Every piece of code you write has a purpose and an expected outcome. Logic helps you make sense of the steps needed to reach that outcome. It's what guides you to write code that behaves predictably and reliably.

- ### Analytical Thinking

Analytical thinking is the ability to assess a situation, evaluate options, and make the best choice. When programming, you'll often encounter situations where there are multiple ways to solve a problem. Analytical thinking helps you choose the most efficient, clear, and scalable solution.

Example

Imagine you're building a program that needs to sort a list of numbers. You could use a quick, built-in function, or you could write a custom sorting function from scratch. Analytical thinking helps you weigh the pros and cons to decide the best approach.

Sort a list of

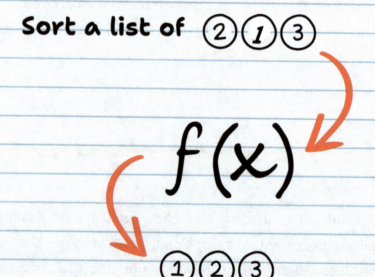

2. Breaking Down Problems into Smaller Parts (Divide and Conquer)

One of the most important skills in programming is the ability to **break down complex problems** into smaller, more manageable parts. This approach is often called **Divide and Conquer**.

- ### Why Divide and Conquer Works

  Tackling a big problem all at once can be overwhelming. But when you break it down into smaller pieces, each piece becomes simpler to understand and solve. Plus, small solutions can be combined to solve the larger problem effectively.

 - ### How to Apply This Approach

  Start by understanding the big picture, then identify the individual tasks needed to reach the end goal. Each task should be simple enough to tackle independently, which keeps you focused and reduces the chances of errors.

Example

Suppose you're writing a program to calculate the average of grades for a class. You could break this task into smaller steps:

Collect all the grades.

Calculate the total sum of the grades.

$$\sum 85 + 90 + 71 = 246$$

Divide the sum by the number of grades to find the average.

$$246 \div 3 = 82$$

By breaking it down, you turn a potentially complex task into a series of manageable steps.

3. Debugging and Iteration as Part of the Learning Process

It's rare that a program is perfect the first time —it's a process! **Debugging** and **iteration** are critical parts of programming and learning to code.

- **Debugging: Finding and Fixing Errors**

Debugging is the process of identifying and fixing issues in your code. Think of it as detective work! When something goes wrong, you need to investigate to find the cause and make adjustments. Debugging teaches you to be detail-oriented and patient.

QUICK
TIPS

Don't be discouraged by bugs! They're a normal part of coding, and every bug you fix makes you a better programmer.

• **Iteration: Improving and Refining Your Code**

Iteration means making small changes, testing, and improving your code gradually. It's rare for a program to be perfect on the first try, so iteration allows you to refine and optimize over time.

Example

$f(x)$

Say you've written a function that works, but it's a bit slow. Through iteration, you can try new methods to make it faster or cleaner, testing each change as you go.

• **Growth Mindset**

Debugging and iteration are exercises in patience, persistence, and adaptability. A growth mindset—believing that skills improve with effort—helps you stay motivated and enjoy the process of learning from your mistakes.

Why This Mindset Matters

Adopting a programmer's mindset of logical thinking, breaking down problems, and embracing debugging as part of the process will set you up for long-term success. Programming is as much about how you think as it is about what you know.

Summary

In this chapter, we explored the importance of logic and analytical thinking, the power of breaking down problems, and the role of debugging and iteration in programming. Developing these skills and habits will make your journey in programming smoother and more rewarding!

1.6 What is Python and why should i learn Python

Python is one of the most popular programming languages today, loved by beginners and professionals alike. In this section, we'll explore Python's history, unique features, and why it's such a valuable language to learn!!!!

Welcome to the world of Python ‼️

1. Brief History and Evolution of Python

Python was created by **Guido van Rossum** and was first released in the early **1990s**. Guido designed Python to be an **easy-to-read** and **easy-to-use** language, aimed at reducing the complexity of programming.

Where the name comes from?

Python isn't named after the snake! Guido was a fan of the British comedy series **Monty Python's Flying Circus** and wanted the language to be fun and accessible, just like the show

Evolution and Growth

Over the years, Python has grown and evolved, with major releases like Python 2 and Python 3. Each version brought new features and improvements, keeping Python modern and powerful. Today, Python 3 is the main version used worldwide.

36

2. Key Features of Python: Readability, Simplicity, and Versatility

Python stands out from other languages because of its unique design and features

Readability

Python's syntax (the rules for writing code) is clear and straightforward, almost like writing in plain English. This makes it easier to read and understand, even for beginners.

Simplicity

Python was designed to be simple. It uses whitespace (like indentation) to structure code, which reduces the need for extra symbols and makes it clean and organized.

Versatility

Python can be used for a wide range of tasks, from web development to data science to artificial intelligence. Its versatility is one of the reasons it's so popular!

3. How Python is used across Industries

Python stands out from other languages because of its unique design and features

Web Development

Frameworks like **Django** and **Flask** allow developers to create powerful, dynamic websites quickly.

Data Science

Python has become the go-to language for data scientists, thanks to libraries like **Pandas**, **NumPy**, and **Matplotlib**, which make data analysis and visualization easy.

Artificial Intelligence and Machine Learning

Python powers cutting-edge AI and ML applications. Libraries like **TensorFlow** and **PyTorch** enable developers to build complex machine-learning models.

Automation

From automating repetitive tasks to handling data pipelines, Python is widely used for scripting and automation across many fields.

4. Advantages for Beginners: Easy Syntax and Strong Community Support

Python is an excellent choice for beginners because it's both easy to learn and well-supported by a vibrant community.

Easy Syntax

Python's syntax is designed to be beginner-friendly, which allows new programmers to focus on learning concepts rather than getting bogged down by complex code.

Strong Community Support

Python has a massive, active community. This means there are plenty of resources, tutorials, forums, and libraries available to help you learn and solve problems. The Python community is known for being welcoming and helpful to beginners

5. Career Opportunities and Demand for Python Skills

Python is one of the most in-demand programming languages in today's job market, offering numerous career opportunities

High Demand in Tech Roles

Python is essential for roles in data science, AI, web development, and software engineering. Companies value Python skills due to its flexibility and the broad range of applications it supports.

Great for Freelancers and Entrepreneurs

Python's ease of use and versatility make it a favorite for freelancers and entrepreneurs. It's a powerful tool for building projects, automating tasks, and even launching startups.

Python consistently ranks among the **top programming languages** for job demand, and it's especially popular in fields that are growing, like AI and data science.

Python is even used in fields like **biology, finance, and astronomy**, making it a truly universal language!

Compare Python's **simplicity** to other languages—where you might need multiple lines of code in other languages, Python can often accomplish the same thing in just one or two lines!

SUMMARY

We explored what makes Python so special and why it's a **fantastic language** to learn. With its readability, simplicity, and wide range of uses, Python is an ideal choice for beginners and professionals alike. From web development to AI, Python opens doors to countless opportunities! below is a mindmap of this section

Key Features of Python: Readability, Simplicity, and Versatility

Brief History and Evolution of Python

What is Python, and Why Should I Learn It?

How Python is Used Across Industries

Advantages for Beginners: Easy Syntax and Strong Community Support

Career Opportunities and Demand for Python Skills

QUIZ

1. What is one advantage of programming a task for a machine?

a) Machines perform tasks slower but more creatively

b) Machines make tasks unnecessarily complex

c) Machines efficiently handle repetitive and complex tasks

d) Machines can work without clear instructions

2.Fill in the Blanks

- _____ languages are closer to human languages and easier to understand.

- _____ and Machine Code are examples of low-level languages.

Exercise

Create a flowchart for deciding whether to study programming or play a game. Use symbols like ovals, rectangles, and diamonds.

Next Up

Ready to start coding? In the next chapter, we'll jump into Python's basic syntax and write our first program together!

Find all the answers for the quiz in the answer key provided at the end! For exercise solutions, check out our support at Github!

Getting Started
with
🐍 PYTHON

What are we going to learn?

1. Installing Python and Setting Up an Environment
2. Writing Your First Python Program
3. Understanding IDEs (Integrated Development Environments)

> Welcome to the start of your Python journey! Before we dive into coding, let's get Python installed and set up an environment for writing our code. With just a few steps, you'll be ready to run your first Python program and explore everything this versatile language has to offer!

2.1 Installing Python and Setting Up an Environment

Before we dive into the installation and setup, remember that if you need a bit of extra help after reading the installation and setup steps, you can check out our GitHub page for detailed guides or watch some YouTube videos on Python installation and setup. We're here to make sure you get off to a smooth start! links are mentioned in **How to get most out of this book** page at the beginning of the book

And remember, all the resources and code files for this content are available on our GitHub! So if you need any files or extra help, feel free to check it out.

1. Installing Python

First things first, let's install Python on your computer. This might feel a bit hectic if you are new to it. But trust me, you'll thank yourself for the sense of accomplishment once you've done it all on your own.

Step 1: Download Python

Head over to the official Python website and download the latest version of Python. Python is compatible with Windows, macOS, and Linux, so choose the right version for your system.

Step 2: Install Python

Once downloaded, open the installer. When you see the setup window, be sure to check the box labeled "Add Python to PATH." This is essential as it allows you to run Python from the command line. Then, click "Install Now." And just like that, Python is installed!

Step 3: Verify Your Installation

To make sure everything is working, open your command line (Terminal on macOS/Linux or Command Prompt on Windows) and type:

```
Terminal   python --version
```

If Python is installed correctly, you should see the version number displayed. Congrats! You're ready to start coding.

2. Setting Up a Python Environment

A Python environment is where your code lives, along with any specific tools or libraries it needs. Setting up a dedicated environment helps keep your projects organized and prevents conflicts between different packages.

Example of a Python Environment

Imagine you're working on two projects:

Project A needs pandas version 1.0.

Project B requires pandas version 1.3.

By creating separate environments, you can install the required version for each project without conflict, allowing both to run smoothly.

49

Creating a Virtual Environment:

Using virtual environments is a common practice in Python development. Here's how to set one up:

In your command line, navigate to the folder where you want your project to live.

Terminal

```
python -m venv myenv
```

This command creates a folder named myenv with a clean Python environment.

Activating the Environment:

To start using your new environment, you'll need to activate it:

On Windows cmd (command prompt) execute below line:

Terminal

```
myenv\Scripts\activate
```

On macOS/Linux:
Terminal
```
source myenv/bin/activate
```

Once activated, you'll see (myenv) in your command prompt or terminal. Now, any libraries you install will only apply to this specific project.

50

2.2 Writing Your First Python Program

Time to write some code! Let's start with a simple "Hello, World!" program—an essential first step for every programmer.

1. Open a text editor (or an IDE, which we'll discuss soon).

2. Type the following:

```python
print("Hello, World!")
```

The print function allows you to display anything in the console or output window. It's a simple command, but it's where all great programmers begin!

3. Save the file as hello.py.

Running Your Code:

In your command line, navigate to where hello.py is saved. In windows you navigate to a location; lets say to Documents folder in cmd like this:

```
Terminal  cd C:\Users\YourUsername\Documents
```

Whereas in mac, you can navigate to a location on terminal like this:

```
Terminal  cd /Users/YourUsername/Documents
```

And on linux, below is the syntax to navigate:

```
Terminal  cd /home/YourUsername/Documents
```

Once you are at the folder which contains the python file, type:

```
python hello.py
```

You should see **"Hello, World!"** printed on the screen. Congratulations—you've written and run your first Python program!

2.3 Understanding IDEs (Integrated Development Environments)

To make coding even smoother, you can use an IDE (Integrated Development Environment). An IDE is like a super-powered text editor designed specifically for coding. It often includes helpful features like:

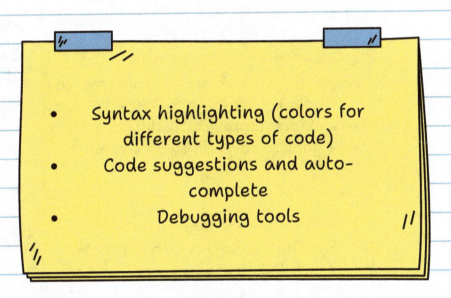

- Syntax highlighting (colors for different types of code)
- Code suggestions and auto-complete
- Debugging tools

⭐Popular Python IDEs

VS Code: Free and highly customizable, VS Code is popular for Python (and almost any other language!). With extensions, you can turn it into a powerful Python environment.

53

PyCharm: A dedicated Python IDE with many built-in tools for coding, testing, and debugging.

 Jupyter Notebook: Great for data science, Jupyter lets you write code in cells, making it easy to test and visualize code snippets.

Each IDE has its own strengths, so try a few and see which fits your style best. The right IDE can make a world of difference as you start coding more complex projects.

If you need more guidance at this step, you can visit our GitHub page for detailed steps where we walk through IDE installations. We've got you covered, every step of the way!

Pro Tip: Don't stress too much about which IDE to use. Try a few and see which one feels right for you. You'll find your rhythm soon enough!

The more you practice code, the more you'll realize that coding is like learning a new language. Stick with it, and you'll be building impressive projects in no time!

Summary

You're all set up! With Python installed, a virtual environment ready, and your first code successfully run, you're prepared for more Python adventures. Get comfortable with your environment and IDE—you'll be spending a lot of time here as you build and explore.

Find all the answers for the quiz in the answer key provided at the end!

QUIZ

1. How can you verify if Python was installed correctly?

a) Open your IDE and check the Python version

b) Type python -m pip in the terminal

c) Type python --version in the command line

d) Open Python IDE

2. What command do you use to create a virtual environment named myenv?

a) python create venv myenv

b) python -m myenv create

c) python -m venv myenv

d) create venv python myenv

For exercise solutions, check out our support at Github!

Exercise

Write a program to print 'My first python program!'

✨ **Next Up:** Let's dive deeper into Python's syntax and get hands-on with data types, variables, and functions!

Basic
Python Syntax

What are we going to learn?

1. Python Syntax and Indentation
2. Comments and Docstrings
3. Running Python Code in the Interpreter vs. Script

You're about to discover what makes Python so approachable and fun to use. Let's dive into the essentials, like indentation, comments, and running your code. This is where the magic of coding really starts to unfold!

3.1 Python Syntax and Indentation

Python has a unique approach to organizing code: it uses indentation rather than braces **{}** that many other programming languages do . This makes it clear and easy to follow. Think of indentation as Python's way of creating "neat stacks" of code that define the structure of your programs.

An indentation is the space at the beginning of a line

```
def greet():
    print("Hello, World!")  # This line is
indented with 4 spaces
```

Notice how the **print** statement is indented under **def greet()**? That indentation tells Python it's part of the **greet** function, and it is written inside it. Keeping your indentation consistent is key, so you won't be wrestling with syntax errors later. Clean code = happy code!

Why Python Uses Indentation:

By using indentation, Python promotes code that's readable and easy to understand. You'll find that sticking to these clean structures makes your code look polished, almost like writing out your thoughts. And it's a great habit to build as you grow in your coding journey!

Did you know that Python's use of indentation is inspired by the importance of readability in software development? It helps avoid "spaghetti code" (code that's hard to follow and maintain).

Always use spaces instead of tabs for indentation to avoid errors and ensure your code is universally readable. The standard is 4 spaces per indentation level.

3.2 Comments and Docstrings

Comments are like notes-to-self or explanations for others who read your code. In Python, adding **#** creates a single-line comment, and it's ignored by Python when running the code. Think of comments as little helpers to make your code clear and understandable.

Example of a Single-Line Comment:

```python
# This comment describes what the next line does
print("Hello, Python!")
```

Docstrings for Function Documentation

Docstrings are next-level comments, used for functions, classes, and modules. They're surrounded by triple quotes (""" ... """) and act as a reference for others using your code. A well-placed docstring can make even the most complex code simple to follow.

61

Example of a Docstring in a Function:

```python
def add_numbers(a, b):
    """
    This function adds two numbers.
    Parameters:
        a (int or float): First number
        b (int or float): Second number
    Returns:
        int or float: The sum of a and b
    """

    return a + b
```

Docstrings make your code shine with clarity. When you return to this function in the future or share it with others, the docstring will be a guide.

Fun Fact: The official Python documentation itself uses docstrings! They help keep code organized and are a great resource for learning how to use Python's built-in features.

3.3 Running Python Code: Interpreter vs. Script

You can run Python code in two main ways: in the *interpreter* or as a *script*. Each has its perks and knowing both will make you versatile and ready to code anywhere!

Running Code in the Interpreter:

- The interpreter is your instant feedback buddy! Type **python** (or **python3** depending on your python version) in the terminal, hit enter, and you're ready to write and test any line of code.
- Ideal for quick experiments and trying out new concepts.

Example in the Interpreter:

Terminal
```
>>> print("Hello from the interpreter!")
Hello from the interpreter!
```

63

Running Code as a Script:

- For larger projects, save your code in a file with a .py extension and run it as a script.
- Perfect for projects you'll revisit or share, and it's great for automating tasks.

Example Script (hello.py):

```
# hello.py
print("Hello from the script!")
```

Run it in the terminal like this:

```
python hello.py
```
Terminal

Use the interpreter to try new things on the fly, and switch to scripts for full-scale projects. It's a winning combination!

> **Fun Fact:** If you save a file as a .py, you're basically telling your computer, "Hey, I'm about to write some Python magic!" 🧙

QUICK TIPS

When working with scripts, keep your files organized! Consider using project folders to group your scripts, data files, and resources. It'll save you a ton of time in the long run.

Summary

Congrats! You've learned about Python's syntax, indentation, comments, and ways to run your code. These foundations set you up to write clear, readable, and organized code—qualities that are key to great programming.

1. In the following code, which line(s) are correctly indented for the function to work properly?

```python
def greet():
print("Hello, World!")
```

a) Both lines are correctly indented

b) Only the def greet() line is correct

c) The print line needs to be indented under def

d) Neither line is correct

Find all the answers for the quiz in the answer key provided at the end!

2. What is the purpose of a docstring in a Python function?

a) To make the function private

b) To document what the function does for future reference

c) To execute code faster

d) To replace comments

For exercise solutions, check out our support at Github!

Exercise

Write a Python function using proper indentation, add comments and a docstring, and practice running the code in both the interpreter and as a script.

✨ **Next Up:** Ready to get hands-on with data? Next, we'll explore variables, data types, and how to manage information in Python. Let's keep the momentum going!

Chap. 4

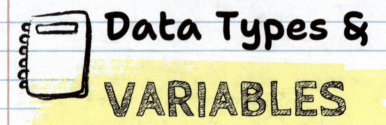

Data Types & VARIABLES

What are we going to learn?

1. Variables and Constants
2. Basic Data Types: Integers, Floats, Strings, Booleans
3. Type Conversion
4. Working with User Input

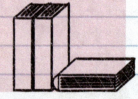

Are you ready to give your code some memory? Let's explore the heart of programming with Python's data types and variables! These are the tools that let us store and work with information, making our programs dynamic and interactive. Ready to turn numbers and text into powerful code?

Let's go!

4.1 Variables and Constants

Variables

A **variable** is like a container that holds data, allowing you to store values and reuse them throughout your code. Variables make your code flexible—just update the variable, and your code will reflect the new value wherever it's used. In Python, you create a variable simply by assigning it a value with =, and Python determines its type automatically.

Example of a Variable:

```
age = 25
name = "Alice"
```

Constants

A **constant** is a value that shouldn't change throughout your program. Python doesn't have built-in constants, but by convention, we write constants in all uppercase letters to indicate they are meant to stay the same.

Example of a Constant:

```
PI = 3.14159
```

 While Python won't enforce it, naming constants in all caps is a good habit—it makes your intentions clear!

FUN FACT

Did you know that in the early days of computing, variables were seen as a kind of "memory drawer"? Just like you store socks in one drawer and t-shirts in another, variables store values in your computer's memory!

Pro Tip: Give your variables meaningful names. Instead of just calling a variable x or y, try names like age, score, or userName. It'll make your code easier to read and understand later on.

4.2 Basic Data Types: Integers, Floats, Strings, Booleans

Python has several basic data types that allow you to store different kinds of data. Here's a quick overview of the essentials:

Integers (int): Whole numbers as well as negative numbers like 42 or -5.

Floats (float): Decimal numbers, like 3.14 or 0.99.

Strings (str): Text data, enclosed in quotes, like "Hello, world!".

Booleans (bool): Represents True or False, which are helpful for logic and decision-making.

Example of Each Data Type:

```
age = 30              # Integer
height = 5.9          # Float
name = "Alice"        # String
is_student = True     # Boolean
```

The Boolean data type (True/False) is named after George Boole, a 19th-century mathematician who laid the groundwork for modern logic and computer science! It might just look like two values, but booleans are behind many of the "yes or no" decisions in your code.

Pro Tip:
Floats can sometimes be a bit tricky when it comes to accuracy. Due to how computers store decimals, calculations like 0.1 + 0.2 might not be exactly 0.3! Keep this in mind when working with decimals that require high precision.

Sometimes, you'll need to convert data from one type to another. Python makes it easy with **type conversion** functions like int(), float(), str(), and bool(). Type conversion is especially useful when combining different types in a single expression or working with user input.

Example of Type Conversion:

```
age = "25"          # Age is a string

age = int(age)      # Convert age to an integer

height = 5.7

height_str = str(height)  # Convert float to
string

height_str = "5.7"
```

⭐ **This flexibility is powerful—Python lets you work with different data types in a way that feels intuitive and adaptable!**

Type conversion is so powerful that Python allows you to combine text and numbers! This is called **casting**, and it's why you can convert 42 (an integer) into "42" (a string). It's super useful when displaying numbers within text or handling user input.

Pro Tip: Type conversion isn't just for user input. Imagine you're working with age data, and you want to add a user's age to a message. By converting age from an integer to a string, you can easily display it within a text message: "You're " + str(age) + " years old!".

You can even convert some strings directly to booleans. For example, bool("Hello") will return True, while bool("") (an empty string) will return False. Empty values in Python are often treated as False.

75

4.4 Working with User Input

Making your program interactive? Python's input() function lets you gather data from the user, making your program more dynamic. By default, input() returns data as a string, so you may need to convert it to the desired type.

Example of Type Conversion:

```python
name = input("What's your name? ")        # Stores the name as a string

age = input("How old are you? ")          # Stores age as a string

age = int(age)                            # Convert age to an integer

print(f"Hello, {name}! You're {age} years old.")
```

QUICK TIPS

When prompting users, be descriptive. Instead of just asking for "Input age: ", try something friendlier like, "How old are you?" It's a small touch, but it makes your program feel more inviting!

Summary

Great job! You've mastered variables, constants, data types, type conversions, and user input. These are core skills that unlock endless possibilities as you build more complex programs.

Can you answer these?

1. Which of the following is a convention in Python for declaring a constant?

a) Using lowercase letters, like pi
b) Prefixing with const, like const pi = 3.14
c) Using uppercase letters, like PI
d) Using a special keyword constant

2. What type of data is stored in the variable price = 19.99?

a) Integer
b) Float
c) String
d) Boolean

3. Which of these would correctly store a Boolean value?

a) is_open = "True"
b) is_open = true
c) is_open = True
d) is_open = "False"

4. If age = "30" is a string, which of the following would convert age to an integer?

a) int.age()
b) float(age)
c) int(age)
d) str(age)

==Find all the answers for the quiz in the answer key provided at the end!==

Quick Exercise

Write a program that prompts the user for their name, age, and height, performs type conversions, and prints a personalized message using the information collected.

For exercise solutions, check out our support at Github!

Next Up: Ready to take your coding to the next level? In the upcoming chapter, we'll dive into operators and expressions. From arithmetic and logical operators to understanding precedence, you'll gain the tools to make your code calculate, compare, and decide like a pro. Let's keep building step by step!

Operators and Expressions

What are we going to learn?

1. Arithmetic Operators
2. Comparison and Logical Operators
3. Assignment and Compound Assignment
4. Operator Precedence

Now it's time to put your code to work with operators! Operators give you the power to calculate, compare, and assign values, turning your program into a smart decision-maker. Let's explore how Python's operators and expressions make all of this possible.

5.1 Arithmetic Operators

Arithmetic Operators

Arithmetic operators are the foundation for calculations in Python. You can add, subtract, multiply, and divide numbers, just like a calculator— but with Python's flexibility to handle complex expressions!

Basic Arithmetic Operators in Python:

- **+ (Addition): Combines values.**
- **- (Subtraction): Finds the difference between values.**
- *** (Multiplication): Multiplies values.**
- **/ (Division): Divides values, returning a float.**
- **// (Floor Division): Divides and rounds down the result to the nearest whole number.**
- **% (Modulus): Returns the remainder of a division.**
- **** (Exponentiation): Raises one number to the power of another.**

81

Example:

```
x = 10
y = 3
print(x + y)   # 13
print(x - y)   # 7
print(x * y)   # 30
print(x / y)   # 3.333...
print(x // y)  # 3
print(x % y)   # 1
print(x ** y)  # 1000
```

These operators are like your toolbox for doing math in Python! Use them to transform numbers, manipulate data, and solve problems.

> **Tip:** Floor division (**//**) can be super helpful when working with integers only. Instead of rounding down manually, it takes care of it for you—perfect for scenarios where you need only whole numbers, like splitting items equally among people.

5.2 Comparison and Logical Operators

Comparison and Logical Operators

To make decisions in your code, Python offers comparison and logical operators. Comparison operators evaluate relationships between values, while logical operators combine multiple conditions. If result of a comparison is positive or in favor then we get true as output else we get false.

Comparison Operators:

==: Checks if two values are equal.
!=: Checks if two values are not equal.
>: Checks if the left value is greater.
<: Checks if the left value is smaller.
>=: Checks if the left value is greater or equal.
<=: Checks if the left value is smaller or equal.

Logical Operators:

- **and:** Returns True if both conditions are true.
- **or:** Returns True if at least one condition is true.
- **not:** Reverses the truth value.

Example:

```python
age = 20
is_student = True
print(age > 18 and is_student)   # True
print(age < 18 or is_student)    # True
print(not is_student)            # False
```

These operators are like your program's sense of judgment. They allow you to create expressions that help Python **"think"** and make decisions.

+

+Fun Fact: Logical operators like and and or form the building blocks of artificial intelligence! By making decisions based on multiple conditions, these operators mimic the way humans make "if-then" decisions.

5.3 Assignment and Compound Assignment Operators

✏️ Assignment and Compound Assignment Operators

In Python, assignment operators assign values to variables. You're already familiar with the = operator, but Python also offers compound assignment operators, which combine an operation and assignment in one step.

Basic Assignment Operators:

- = Assigns a value to a variable.

Use = and == carefully! If you need to check if two things are exactly the same, == is your friend. But be cautious, == checks for equality, while = is for assignment. Mixing them up is a common "gotcha" for new programmers.

Compound Assignment Operators:

+=: Adds and assigns (e.g., x += 5 is equivalent to x = x + 5).
-=: Subtracts and assigns.
*=: Multiplies and assigns.
/=: Divides and assigns (result is a float).
//=: Floor-divides and assigns.
%=: Modulus and assigns.
**=: Exponentiates and assigns.

Example:

```
count = 10
count += 5   # count is now 15
count -= 2   # count is now 13
count *= 3   # count is now 39
```

These operators let you streamline your code by updating variable values without rewriting expressions. They're a great time-saver!

FACT

Compound assignment operators are like shortcuts! Imagine you're tallying up a score in a game. Instead of typing score = score + 10, you can just write score += 10. It's a mini time-saver with every line.

Tip: When working with these operators, start with simple tasks, like updating a counter. Once you're comfortable, compound assignment operators will feel like second nature, helping keep your code clean and compact.

Pro Tip: Compound operators work with strings too! You can use += to build strings without starting from scratch each time. For example, greeting += " world!" would add to your original greeting.

5.4 Operator Precedence

Operator Precedence

When working with multiple operators in a single expression, Python follows a specific order called operator precedence. Some operators have a higher "rank" and are evaluated first.

Here's a simple order to keep in mind:

- **Parentheses:** ()
- **Exponentiation:** **
- **Multiplication, Division, Floor Division, Modulus:** *, /, //, %
- **Addition and Subtraction:** +, –

Example of Precedence:

```python
result = 3 + 2 * 4 ** 2 / 2 - 5
print(result)  # 14.0
```

Breaking it down: Python first evaluates **4 ** 2** (exponentiation), then **2 * 16**, then division, and finally the addition and subtraction.

Fun Fact: Python's operator precedence is a lot like math's **PEMDAS** rules (Parentheses, Exponents, Multiplication/Division, Addition/Subtraction). Python even lets you use parentheses to control the order, so your code reads just how you intend it! Try this mini-phrase to remember the order: **"Please Excuse My Dear Aunt Sally,"** which stands for Parentheses, Exponentiation, Multiplication, Division, Addition, and Subtraction.

Tip: When in doubt, use parentheses to clarify! Even if you know the rules, parentheses can make complex expressions easier to read and reduce the chances of errors.

Summary
You're all set! With arithmetic, comparison, logical, and assignment operators in your toolkit, you can write code that calculates, compares, and even makes decisions based on complex expressions.

QUIZ

Find all the answers for the quiz in the answer key provided at the end!

1. What will this code print?
```
x = 10
y = 20
print(x > 5 and y < 25)
```

a) True

b) False

c) 0

d) 1

2 Which of the following statements is correct about the += operator?

a) x += y is the same as x = y + x

b) x += y is the same as x = x + y

c) x += y is the same as x = x - y

d) x += y is the same as x = x / y

Exercise

Write a Python program that calculates a total cost based on the quantity and price input by the user and applies a discount of 10%.

For exercise solutions, check out our support at Github!

✨ **Next Up:** Ready to bring your program to life with decisions and actions? In the next chapter, we'll dive into conditional statements and loops, where your program gets interactive and responsive. Exciting stuff ahead!

Control Flow Statements

What are we going to learn?

1. Conditional Statements: if, elif, and else
2. Loops: while and for Loops
3. Nested Loops
4. break, continue, and pass Statements

Time to give your Python code some serious decision-making power! Control flow statements let your program take different actions based on conditions or repeat tasks until a certain goal is reached. Imagine your code as a train, and control flow statements are the tracks that guide it—switching, looping, and even skipping steps to get exactly where it needs to go.

Let's jump into the essentials of controlling the flow of your code with confidence.

6.1 Conditional Statements: if, elif, and else

> **Conditional Statements: if, elif, and else**
>
> Conditional statements are the "if this, then do that" logic that makes your code responsive and smart. Python uses if, elif, and else statements to check conditions and decide what to do next.

- **if**: Checks a condition. If it's true, Python runs the code under 'if'.
- **elif (short for "else if")**: Adds more conditions to check if the initial 'if' was false.
- **else**: Catches anything that wasn't true in 'if' or 'elif'.

Example:

```python
temperature = 25

if temperature > 30:
    print("It's hot outside!")
elif temperature > 20:
    print("It's warm.")
else:
    print("It's chilly.")
```

Think of these statements like road signs, guiding your code down the right path based on the conditions it encounters. Easy, right?

Tip: Use **elif** instead of multiple **if**s to make your code run faster! Python always checks each **if** condition individually, but with **elif**, the following conditions are only evaluated if the previous **if** or **elif** was not satisfied. This way, once a true condition is found, Python skips the rest, making the code more efficient.

Pro Tip: Always include an **else** in your conditions if there's a logical "**last resort**" case. This not only covers every possible outcome but can also make your code more understandable to others

6.2 Loops: while and for Loops

Loops: while and for Loops

Loops allow you to repeat tasks without rewriting code. You can use them to cycle through data, automate tasks, or simply repeat instructions until a goal is reached.

while Loop

A **while** loop repeats as long as a condition is true. It's perfect when you don't know exactly how many times the loop should run.

Example:

```
count = 0
while count < 5:
    print("Count is:", count)
    count += 1
```

Tip: Watch out for infinite while loops! If you forget to update the condition inside, for example if you don't increment the count in above example, the value of count will always remain less than 5 and your loop will never stop. Adding a print statement in early testing can help spot endless loops fast!

for Loop

A for loop is ideal when you know how many times to repeat a task or when you want to go through each item in a collection, like a list.

Example:

```python
fruits = ["apple", "banana", "cherry"]
for fruit in fruits:
    print("I like", fruit)
```

It says : execute the code inside this loop for each fruit present in the fruits list

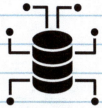

By the way, you might have noticed a list called **fruits** in the example above. Don't worry if you're not entirely sure about it right now! We'll be diving into lists and other data structures in more details later. For now, just know that lists are one way to store multiple items and this for loop here is running for each fruit present inside the list and then printing something for each fruit!.

Each loop has its purpose, so pick the one that fits your task. Remember, loops are powerful tools that help you work smarter, not harder!

6.3 Nested Loops

Nested Loops

Sometimes you'll need a loop inside another loop, especially when working with grids, matrices, or nested data structures. Nested loops let you tackle complex problems step by step.

Example:

```
for i in range(1, 4):     # Outer loop
    for j in range(1, 4):   # Inner loop
        print(i, j)
```

Imagine a nested loop like a team of people each doing their job within a project, and that project is again part of a larger project. This outer loop sets up the main task or objective, and the inner loop completes detailed work within each smaller project.

98

In the above example, if there are 4 large projects, the inner loop means that each of those 4 larger projects contains 4 smaller projects, and when we sum all the smaller projects, the result is 4 x 4 = 16 smaller projects. This means the nested for-loop will run for a total of 16 times.

Fun Fact: Nested loops are like layers of a cake. They're great for handling multi-layered tasks, like rows and columns in a grid or pixels in an image. For example, when processing images, each pixel's row and column are often handled by a nested loop.

Tip: Be cautious with nested loops. The deeper you nest, the more computationally expensive it gets. In cases of three or more levels, see if there's a way to reduce nesting —it'll make your code faster and cleaner.

6.4 break, continue, and pass Statements

Python gives you tools to control your loops further with **break**, **continue**, and **pass**.

break: Exits the loop immediately, ending it.

continue: Skips the rest of the current loop iteration and moves to the next one.

pass: Does nothing—it's a placeholder when you need to include a line but don't want any action.

The number till which the sequence goes (exclusive, i.e., it won't include this number) for the range function

Example:

```python
for i in range(5):
    if i == 2:
        continue    # Skips printing 2
    print(i)
```

These statements are like remote controls for your loop, allowing you to stop, skip, or pause as needed. They make your code even more adaptable to different scenarios.

Tip: break is especially handy for loops where you're searching for a specific item, like finding the first occurrence of something in a list. It stops the loop as soon as you find what you're looking for, saving time.

Pro Tip: continue can be a lifesaver when you only want to process items that meet certain conditions. Place it early in your loop to skip items that don't match, making your code more efficient.

Summary
Great job! You've just gained control over how your code flows, making it smart, responsive, and efficient. With conditional statements and loops, your programs can make decisions, repeat tasks, and even pause or skip steps when necessary.

QUIZ

1. What will this code output?

```python
for i in range(5):
    if i == 3:
        pass
    else:
        print(i)
```

a) 0 1 2 4

b) 0 1 2 3 4

c) 1 2 3 4

d) Error

Find all the answers for the quiz in the answer key provided at the end!

2. Which of the following keywords would you use if you want to skip the current iteration and continue with the next iteration?

a) pass

b) continue

c) break

d) return

Exercise

Write a number-guessing game where the program chooses a number, and the user has to guess it.

For exercise solutions, check out our support at Github!

Hint:

1. Set a secret number, e.g., secret_number = 7.
2. Use a while loop to repeatedly ask the user to guess the number.
3. If the guess is too high, print "Too high!" and continue.
4. If the guess is too low, print "Too low!" and continue.
5. If the guess is correct, print "Congratulations! You guessed it!" and exit the loop.

Bonus: Use the break statement to exit the loop once the user guesses correctly.

Next Up: Get ready to work with functions—Python's way of bundling tasks into reusable code blocks. Functions will make your code cleaner, faster, and easier to manage!

Functions & MODULES

What are we going to learn?

1. Defining Functions
2. Parameters and Return Values
3. Scope and Lifetime of Variables
4. Built-in Functions vs. User-defined Functions
5. Importing and Using Modules

Now that you've got a solid foundation in Python, it's time to enhance your coding workflow by mastering functions—the key to writing efficient, reusable code. Functions and modules are like the building blocks that help you organize and reuse code, making your programs cleaner, more efficient, and easier to manage. Imagine you're putting together a puzzle, and each piece is a function. When you combine them, you create something much bigger than the individual pieces!

7.1 Defining Functions

A function in Python is a way to group a set of instructions together. You can call that function whenever you need it, instead of rewriting the same code multiple times. This makes your code cleaner, faster, and way more organized!

To define a function, use the def keyword, followed by the function name and parentheses:

```python
def greet():
    print("Hello, welcome to Python!")
```

Example:

```python
def say_hello(name):
    print(f"Hello, {name}!")

say_hello("Alice")   # Output: Hello, Alice!
say_hello("Bob")     # Output: Hello, Bob!
```

FUN FACT

Did you know? The first function ever created was in the 17th century by a mathematician named Blaise Pascal! Now, functions are a key part of modern programming.

7.2 Parameters and Return Values

Functions can take parameters (values you give it) and return values (results the function gives back). This makes functions super powerful because they can work with different inputs and produce different outputs!

Parameters: Values you send into the function.

Return: The result the function gives back to you.

Example:

```python
def add_numbers(a, b):
    return a + b

result = add_numbers(3, 4)
print(result)  # Output: 7
```

Tip: You can think of parameters as ingredients for a recipe, and the return value is the final dish you get!

7.3 Scope and Lifetime of Variables

Variables inside a function are local, meaning they can only be used inside that function. Outside the function, they don't exist. This is called the scope of a variable.

Local Scope: Variables inside a function.

Global Scope: Variables outside any function, accessible throughout the entire program.

Example:

```python
def greet():
    message = "Hello, World!"  # Local variable
    print(message)

greet()
# print(message)  # This would cause an error
because 'message' is local to the function
```

7.4 Built-in Functions vs. User-defined Functions

Python comes with tons of built-in functions that you can use right away, like print(), len(), and type(). These functions are pre-defined in Python, so you don't have to create them yourself.

But what if you need a function for a specific task? That's when you write your own user-defined functions, just like we did earlier with add_numbers().

Example of a Built-in Function:

```python
print("Hello, World!")  # Built-in function
```

Example of a User-Defined Function:

```python
def multiply(x, y):
    return x * y
```

Tip: Built-in functions are great for everyday tasks, but user-defined functions give you the freedom to design your own tools for specific problems!

7.5 Importing and Using Modules

Modules are collections of functions and variables that you can use in your programs. Instead of writing everything from scratch, you can import modules and reuse the functionality that others have built. This is like borrowing tools from a toolbox!

To use a module, just use the import keyword:

```
import math
print(math.sqrt(16))  # Output: 4.0
```

You can even import specific functions from a module:

```
from math import sqrt
print(sqrt(25)) # Output: 5.0
```

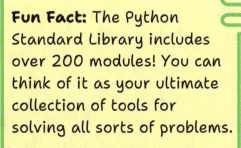

Fun Fact: The Python Standard Library includes over 200 modules! You can think of it as your ultimate collection of tools for solving all sorts of problems.

Summary

Functions and modules are your secret weapons in Python! With functions, you can organize your code into reusable blocks, and with modules, you can access tons of pre-written tools to make your programming life easier. You've just unlocked the power of cleaner, smarter, and more efficient code!

Can you answer these?

1. What does a function return if there is no return statement?

a) 0
b) An error
c) None
d) The last variable in the function

2. Which scope is only accessible inside the function where it's declared?

a) Local scope
b) Global scope
c) Module scope
d) External scope

3. Which of the following is a built-in function in Python?

a) multiply()
b) add_numbers()
c) print()
d) custom_function()

Find all the answers for the quiz in the answer key provided at the end!

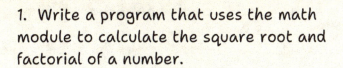

Quick Exercise

1. Write a program that uses the math module to calculate the square root and factorial of a number.

2. Create your own Python module with custom functions.

Steps:

- Create a new file named custom_module.py.
- Define a few functions inside custom_module.py, such as greet() and calculate_area(radius).
- In a separate file, import custom_module and call your functions to verify they work.

For exercise solutions, check out our support at Github!

Next Up: Already comfortable with the basics? Let's now refine your coding skills by mastering data structures—the foundation of efficient programming.

Data Structures

What are we going to learn?

1. Lists: Creating, Accessing, and Modifying
2. Tuples and Immutable Sequences
3. Dictionaries: Key-Value Pairs
4. Sets and Set Operations
5. Working with Data Structures

You've already learned about variables, which are like small boxes where you store a single piece of data—whether it's a number, a word, or a true/false value. But now, let's take it up a notch! Imagine you need to store multiple pieces of data at once. That's where data structures come in!

Data structures are like supercharged variables—they allow you to organize and manage large amounts of data in a more efficient way. Rather than just storing one piece of information, data structures help you store groups of data, all organized in different ways.

115

8.1 Lists: Creating, Accessing, and Modifying

Lists are your go-to when you need to store an ordered collection of data. Think of it as a variable holding multiple values—a collection of items that you can access, modify, or even add to as you go.

- **Creating a List:** Lists are created with square brackets [].

  Accessing Items: You access list items using their index.

  Modifying Items: Lists are mutable, meaning you can change the values inside them.

Example:

```
fruits = ["apple", "banana", "cherry"]
print(fruits[0])  # Output: apple
fruits[1] = "blueberry"  # Modify an item
print(fruits)  # Output: ['apple', 'blueberry', 'cherry']
```

Tip: Lists are flexible—think of them like a toolbox, where you can store different tools and use them whenever needed!

8.2 Tuples and Immutable Sequences

Tuples are just like lists, but with a key difference: they are immutable, meaning you cannot change them once created. This makes them perfect for storing data that shouldn't be altered.

Creating a Tuple: Tuples are created with parentheses ().

Accessing Items: Like lists, you can access items using their index.

Example:

```
coordinates = (10, 20)
print(coordinates[0])  # Output: 10
# coordinates[1] = 30  # This would cause an error, because tuples are immutable
```

8.3 Dictionaries: Key-Value Pairs

> Dictionaries allow you to store data in a key-value pair format, making it super easy to look up a value by its key. Think of it as having a variable that holds a collection of pairs, where each key maps to a specific value.

Creating a Dictionary: Dictionaries are created with curly braces {}.

Accessing Items: You access items using their keys, not an index.

Example:

```
person = {"name": "John", "age": 30}
print(person["name"])  # Output: John
person["age"] = 31  # Modify a value
person["city"] = "New York"  # Add a new key-value pair
print(person)  # Output: {'name': 'John', 'age': 31, 'city': 'New York'}
```

8.4 Sets and Set Operations

Sets are similar to lists, but with one major difference—they store unique, unordered items. If you need a collection where duplicates aren't allowed, sets are your best bet!

Creating a Set:

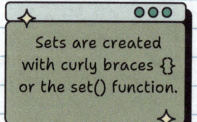

Sets are created with curly braces {} or the set() function.

Operations:

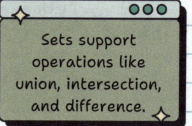

Sets support operations like union, intersection, and difference.

Example:

```python
fruits = {"apple", "banana", "cherry"}
fruits.add("orange")  # Add an item
fruits.remove("banana")  # Remove an item
print(fruits)  # Output: {'apple', 'cherry', 'orange'}
```

Fun Fact: Sets are great for checking if an item is part of a collection, and they are faster than lists for membership testing!

Why sets are faster:

Lists: When you check if an item exists in a list, Python has to go through each item one by one (this is called a linear search), which can be slow for large lists.

Sets: Sets are implemented in a way that allows for much faster membership testing. They use a technique called hashing, which makes checking if an item is in the set much quicker—almost constant time, regardless of how many items are in the set.

8.5 Working with Data Structures

At this point, you've learned about some of Python's most important data structures. The real magic happens when you start using them together—whether you're storing lists inside dictionaries, or combining sets and tuples to tackle more complex problems. Python gives you the freedom to choose the best structure for your data, making your code more efficient and easier to manage.

Tip: As you work on more complex projects, think about which data structure is best suited for the job. A well-chosen data structure can make your code faster and more elegant!

Summary

Congratulations Buddy!, you've just unlocked the power of **data structures** in Python! From lists to sets, each data structure offers a unique way to store and manage your data. Whether you're working with ordered data, key-value pairs, or unique elements, Python has the perfect tool for the job.

Can you answer these?

1. Which of the following methods adds an item to the end of a list?

a) insert()
b) append()
c) add()
d) extend()

2. What will the following code output?

```python
data = {"city": "Paris", "population": 2000000}
data["country"] = "France"
print(data)
```

a) {"city": "Paris", "population": 2000000}
b) {"city": "Paris", "population": 2000000, "country": "France"}
c) {"city": "Paris", "country": "France"}
d) Error

3. Which of the following statements is true about dictionaries?

a) They are ordered collections of elements.
b) Keys in a dictionary can be duplicated.
c) Dictionaries store data in key-value pairs.
d) Dictionaries cannot store numeric values.

Find all the answers for the quiz in the answer key provided at the end!

1.Write a program to store student names and their grades in a dictionary, and calculate the average grade.

Steps:

1. Define a dictionary student_grades with student names as keys and their grades as values.
2. Calculate the average grade of all students.
3. Print each student's name and grade, as well as the average grade.

For exercise solutions, check out our support at Github!

2.Write a function that takes a list of words and returns a set of unique words.

Steps:

1. Define a function get_unique_words(words_list).
2. Inside the function, convert words_list to a set.
3. Return the set of unique words.

Next Up: Time to master String Manipulation! Strings are one of the most versatile data types, and knowing how to manipulate them will give you the power to handle text like a pro! Get ready to learn how to slice, format, and transform strings in ways that will make your code cleaner and more efficient!!

String Manipulation
Unleash the Power of Text!

What are we going to learn?

1. Basic String Operations
2. String Methods and Formatting
3. f-Strings and format()
4. Working with Multiline Strings

Now that you've got the data structures down, let's dive into the world of string manipulation! In Python, strings are super flexible and powerful, and learning how to work with them will make you a pro at handling text, from formatting messages to slicing and dicing strings. Let's break down some key concepts and get you comfortable with string operations!

9.1 Basic String Operations

Basic String Operations
Strings in Python can be manipulated in a variety of ways, and some of the most basic operations are a breeze to use!

Let's start simple:

Concatenation: Combine strings using the **+** operator.
Repetition: Repeat a string with the ***** operator.

```python
greeting = "Hello, "
name = "Alice!"

# Concatenate two strings
message = greeting + name
print(message)  # Output: Hello, Alice!

# Repeat the string 3 times
repeat_hello = "Hello! " * 3

# Output: Hello! Hello! Hello!
print(repeat_hello)
```

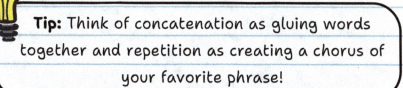

Tip: Think of concatenation as gluing words together and repetition as creating a chorus of your favorite phrase!

9.2 String Methods and Formatting

String Methods and Formatting

Python comes with a ton of built-in string methods that make text manipulation easy. These methods allow you to perform common tasks like changing case, trimming whitespace, and more.

upper(): Converts a string to uppercase.
lower(): Converts a string to lowercase.
strip(): Removes leading and trailing whitespace.
replace(): Replaces a part of the string with another.

Example:

```
text = "  Python is awesome!  "
print(text.upper())  # Output: PYTHON IS
AWESOME!
print(text.strip())  # Output: Python is
awesome!
print(text.replace("awesome", "cool"))  #
Output: Python is cool!
```

Focus on the spaces in the original string and in the output strings!!!

9.3 f-Strings and format()

When it comes to inserting values into strings, Python gives you two powerful tools: **f-strings** (formatted string literals) and the format() method. These make it easy to create dynamic strings with variables or expressions!

- **f-Strings:** Introduced in Python 3.6, f-strings let you embed expressions inside string literals.
- **format():** An older but still very useful way to format strings.

f-String Example:

```python
name = "Bob"
age = 25
greeting = f"Hello, my name is {name} and I am {age} years old."
print(greeting)
# Output: Hello, my name is Bob and I am 25 years old.
```

format() Example:

```python
greeting = "Hello, my name is {} and I am {} years old.".format(name, age)
print(greeting)  # Output: Hello, my name is Bob and I am 25 years old.
```

Tip: f-strings are faster and more readable, but format() is still a great option for older versions of Python or more complex formatting.

9.4 Working with Multiline Strings

Sometimes, you'll need to work with multiline strings—strings that span more than one line. Python makes this easy using triple quotes (""" or '''), which allow you to include line breaks directly in your string.

Multiline Strings: Simply enclose your text in triple quotes to preserve formatting and line breaks.

Example:

```python
poem = """Roses are red,
Violets are blue,
Python is awesome,
And so are you!"""
print(poem)
```

Output:

```
Roses are red,
Violets are blue,
Python is awesome,
And so are you!
```

Fun Fact: Multiline strings are perfect for writing out large chunks of text like poems, quotes, or even SQL queries.

Summary

You've just learned how to perform some basic string operations and discovered the power of string methods and formatting. Whether you're concatenating strings, changing their case, or embedding dynamic values, Python's string manipulation tools make it easy to work with text. And don't forget about multiline strings—they'll help you handle larger blocks of text with ease!

1. What will the following code output?

```
name = "Alice"
age = 30
print(f"Name: {name}, Age: {age}")
```

a) Name: Alice, Age: 30

b) Name: {name}, Age: {age}

c) Name: Alice Age: 30

d) Error

2. What will the following code output?

```python
word = "Python"
print(word * 3)
```

a) PythonPythonPython

b) Python Python Python

c) Error

d) 3 Python

Find all the answers for the quiz in the answer key provided at the end!

Exercise

Write a function that takes a sentence as input and returns the sentence in uppercase without leading or trailing spaces.

For exercise solutions, check out our support at Github!

Next Up: Get ready to dive into error handling—because even the best code can hit a bump in the road. We'll teach you how to handle errors like a pro and keep your code running smoothly!

Error and Exception Handling

Keeping Your Code Smooth and Bug-Free

What are we going to learn?

1. Types of Errors in Python
2. Try, Except, Else, and Finally
3. Raising Exceptions
4. Common Exception Types

❝ Alright, buddy! Let's talk about something every coder needs to master—not just to keep things running smoothly, but to make sure your code knows when to stop if something's off or isn't safe to execute. We're talking about Error and Exception Handling—the key to catching those "no- go" moments before they mess things up!. No matter how awesome your code is, errors are going to pop up. And when they do, you don't want your program to just crash and burn, right? So, we need a way to catch those errors and tackle them in a smooth, controlled way.

Let's dive in and see how Python helps you do this!

10.1 Types of Errors in Python

Before we handle errors, let's understand the types of errors you might run into.

These errors fall into two categories:

Syntax Errors: These happen when your code doesn't follow Python's rules. For example, missing a parenthesis or forgetting a colon at the end of a **for** loop.

Example: if x > 10 print(x) (Oops! Missing a colon at the end of the **if** statement.)

Exceptions: These occur when something goes wrong while the program is running (but the code is syntactically correct). It could be anything from trying to divide by zero to accessing a file that doesn't exist.

Example: 1 / 0 (Dividing by zero? That's an exception!)

10.2 Try, Except, Else, and Finally: The Power of Control

Now that you know what kind of errors can occur, let's look at how we can catch and handle them. This is where the **try** and **except** blocks come into play.

 Try Block: This is where you put the code that you think might cause an error.

 Except Block: If an error occurs inside the try block, Python jumps to the except block to handle the error.

 Else Block: If no error occurs in the try block, Python will execute the else block.

 Finally Block: This block will run no matter what—whether there was an error or not. It's perfect for cleanup actions like closing files.

10.3 Raising Exceptions: Taking Control

Sometimes, you might want to **raise your own exceptions**. This is useful if something goes wrong that isn't already covered by Python's built-in exceptions. You can **raise an exception** manually using the `raise` keyword.

Example:

```python
def check_age(age):
    if age < 0:
        raise ValueError("Age can't be negative!")
    elif age < 18:
        raise ValueError("You must be at least 18 years old.")
    else:
        print("Welcome to the site!")

# Testing the function
try:
    check_age(-5)
except ValueError as e:
    print(e)
```

In this case, if someone tries to input a negative age, we raise a custom exception with a helpful message.

141

10.4 Common Exception Types

There are a ton of built-in exceptions you'll run into while coding. I'm not going to throw all of them at you right now, but go ahead and take a look by searching for them online when you can —they're pretty cool to know!.

Here are some common ones:

- **ZeroDivisionError:** Happens when you try to divide by zero.
- **FileNotFoundError:** Raised when Python can't find the file you're trying to access.
- **IndexError:** Occurs when you try to access an index in a list that doesn't exist.
- **ValueError:** Raised when a function receives an argument of the correct type but an inappropriate value (like trying to convert a letter to an integer).

Quick Tip: Whenever you catch an exception, it's a good idea to print or log the exception message so you can understand what went wrong and fix it.

Summary

You've now leveled up to handle errors and exceptions like a pro! You learned about the common types of errors, how to use try, except, else, and finally to control your program flow, and how to raise your own exceptions when necessary. Remember, error handling keeps your code from crashing and makes sure your users get a smooth experience.

1. What will the following code output?

```python
try:
    num = int("not_a_number")
except ValueError:
    print("Invalid number!")
else:
    print("Conversion successful!")
finally:
    print("End of program.")
```

a) Invalid number!
   End of program.

b) Conversion successful!
   End of program.

c) Invalid number!
   Conversion successful!

d) End of program.

2. What will the following code output?

```python
def check_age(age):
    if age < 0:
        raise ValueError("Age can't be
negative!")
    else:
        print("Age is valid.")

try:
    check_age(-5)
except ValueError as e:
    print(e)
```

a) Age is valid.

b) -5

c) Age can't be negative!

d) ValueError

Find all the answers for the quiz in the answer key provided at the end!

Exercise

Write a function that prompts the user for a number, then divides 10 by that number. Handle both **ZeroDivisionError** (if the user inputs zero) and **ValueError** (if the input isn't a number).

Hint:

1. Define a function **divide_by_input()**.
2. Use a **try** block to get user input and divide 10 by the input.
3. Catch both **ZeroDivisionError** and **ValueError** with separate **except** blocks.
4. Print an appropriate message for each exception.

Exercise

Write a function that checks if a given age is valid for signing up on a website (age must be at least 18). If the age is less than 18, raise a ValueError with a custom message.

Hint:

1. Define a function validate_age(age).
2. Use an if statement to check if age < 18.
3. Raise a ValueError with the message "You must be at least 18 to sign up!" if the age is less than 18.

For exercise solutions, check out our support at Github!

✨ **Next Up:** Next, we'll take on File Handling! You'll learn how to read from and write to files with ease. Ready to store data, save progress, and unlock new possibilities? Let's turn up the page!

File Handling

Mastering the Art of Managing Files

What are we going to learn?

1. Reading from and Writing to Files
2. Working with Different File Modes
3. Exception Handling in File Operations
4. Using with for File Management

Listen, buddy! The variables we create in our Python application hold data only as long as the program is running and are limited to the scope in which they're defined. But files? They're not just for temporary storage. Files allow us to save data permanently, even after the program stops running. This means, when you store information in a file, it sticks around until you need it again, making your program smarter and more reliable.

One of the coolest features of working with files is that you can **read from other files** as well. These external files might contain all sorts of data—whether it's user input, logs, or configurations—and you can use that data in your program, making your application more dynamic and flexible.

Let's dive in and explore how Python handles file reading and writing, as well as how to manage your file operations safely and effectively!

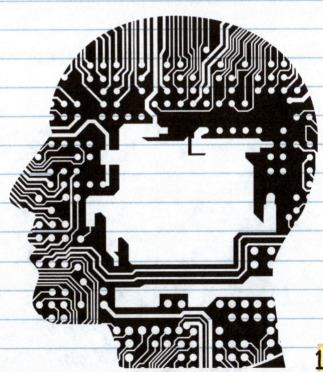

11.1 Reading from and Writing to Files

Python makes working with files super simple. You can open a file, read its contents, and write new data into it—all in just a few lines of code. Whether you're saving user input or reading data for analysis, file handling gives you a lot of control.

- **Reading from a file:** Use the open() function to access a file, then use .read() or .readlines() to get the content.
- **Writing to a file:** Open the file in write mode and use .write() to store data in it.

Example:

```python
# Writing to a file
with open("example.txt", "w") as file:
    file.write("Hello, world!\nWelcome to Python file handling.")



# Reading from a file
with open("example.txt", "r") as file:
    content = file.read()
    print(content)
```

11.2 Working with Different File Modes

Python offers several file modes that determine how a file is accessed. Depending on the task, you can choose the right mode for reading, writing, or appending data.

Here are the most common modes:

"r": Read (opens the file for reading, default mode).

"w": Write (opens the file for writing, creates the file if it doesn't exist).

"a": Append (opens the file for appending new data at the end).

"rb", "wb": Read/Write in binary mode (useful for non-text data).

Example:

```python
# Opening a file in append mode to add more data
with open("example.txt", "a") as file:
    file.write("\nAppended text!")
```

11.3 Exception Handling in File Operations

While working with files, things don't always go as planned. Maybe the file doesn't exist, or you don't have permission to read/write it. That's where **exception handling** comes in.

Using **try-except** blocks, you can catch potential errors and handle them gracefully, without crashing your program.

Example:

```
try:
    with open("nonexistent_file.txt", "r") as file:
        content = file.read()
except FileNotFoundError:
    print("Oops! The file doesn't exist.")
```

Tip: Always wrap file operations in a try-except block to avoid unexpected crashes and ensure smooth user experience!

11.4 Using with for File Management

One of the best practices when handling files is using the with statement. It automatically takes care of closing the file after you're done with it. This way, you don't need to worry about forgetting to close the file and possibly causing memory leaks.

Example:

```
# The 'with' statement automatically handles file closing

with open("example.txt", "r") as file:
    content = file.read()
    print(content)  # File is automatically closed after this block
```

Fun Fact: Using with is like giving your file a personal assistant who ensures it's properly closed without you lifting a finger!

Why File Handling Matters?

So, why should you care about file handling? Well, it allows you to store and manage persistent data that your program can access even after it's been closed. If you need to save user settings, logs, or even large datasets, files are your go-to solution!

You can also read data from other files—these might contain configurations, external inputs, or data that you want to process in your program. For example, you can read a file that holds a user's settings and use those settings in your program without having to ask the user every time.

Summary

You've just learned how to perform some core file operations in Python: reading from and writing to files, using different file modes, handling errors, and making your file management easy with the with statement. With file handling in your toolkit, you can now store and manage data for long-term use, interact with external data, and create more robust programs.

QUIZ

1. What does the following code do?
```
with open("data.txt", "w") as file:
    file.write("Hello, Python!")
```

a) Reads data from data.txt

b) Writes "Hello, Python!" to data.txt and creates it if it doesn't exist

c) Appends "Hello, Python!" to data.txt

d) Opens data.txt in binary mode

2. In a try-except block for file handling, what will this code output if the file doesn't exist?

```
try:
    with open("missing.txt", "r") as file:
        data = file.read()
except FileNotFoundError:
    print("File not found!")
```

a) An error message

b) File not found!

c) IOError

d) None of the above

Find all the answers for the quiz in the answer key provided at the end!

Exercise

Write a program that tries to open a file named data.txt and reads its contents. If the file doesn't exist, catch the FileNotFoundError and print "File not found! Please check the file name."

For exercise solutions, check out our support at Github!

Next Up: Up next, we're diving into **Object-Oriented Programming (OOP)!** We'll explore how to structure your code with **classes** and **objects** to make it cleaner and more efficient. It's time to level up your coding skills!

Object-Oriented Programming (OOP) Basics:

What are we going to learn?

1. Classes and Objects
2. Attributes and Methods
3. Constructors and Destructors
4. Inheritance, Encapsulation, and Polymorphism

Alright, my friend! We've come so far already, and now it's time to level up our coding journey! Ready to dive into Object-Oriented Programming (OOP)? Trust me, this is the kind of stuff that'll take your skills to the next level. OOP is like learning how to organize your thoughts and ideas in the clearest way possible, making your code cleaner, more efficient, and easier to maintain.

Let's jump in and see how we can take our programs to new heights!

12.1 Classes and Objects: The Heart of OOP

So, here's where it gets exciting: classes and objects. Think of a class as a blueprint—like a recipe for creating something cool. The object is the actual thing you create from that recipe. It's like baking a cake: the class is the recipe, and the object is the cake you get at the end!

Example:

```python
class Dog:
    def bark(self):
        print("Woof!")

# Creating an object (instance) of the Dog class
my_dog = Dog()
my_dog.bark()  # Output: Woof!
```

Here, Dog is the class, and my_dog is the object. You can think of bark() as the dog's "action" that we've programmed into the class.

12.2 Attributes and Methods: Adding Personality to Your Objects

Now, let's give our objects some personality! Attributes are like the characteristics of your objects—things that describe them. Methods are what the objects can do—the actions they can perform. By combining these, your objects become more than just data; they come to life!

Example:

```python
class Dog:
    def __init__(self, name, age):
        self.name = name  # Attribute
        self.age = age    # Attribute

    def bark(self):  # Method
        print(f"{self.name} says Woof!")

# Creating an object
my_dog = Dog("Buddy", 3)
my_dog.bark()  # Output: Buddy says Woof!
```

In this example, name and age are attributes, while bark() is a method. The __init__ method is the **constructor**—it's what initializes your object when it's created.

160

12.3 Constructors and Destructors: The Start and End of an Object's Life

Every object has a beginning and an end. When an object is created, the constructor kicks in to set things up. And when it's time to say goodbye, the destructor takes care of the cleanup.

Example:

```python
class Dog:
    def __init__(self, name):
        self.name = name
        print(f"{self.name} is born!")

    def __del__(self):
        print(f"{self.name} is gone!")

# Creating and deleting an object
my_dog = Dog("Buddy")  # Output: Buddy is born!
del my_dog              # Output: Buddy is gone!
```

The __init__ method runs when the object is created, and the __del__ method is called when it's deleted. A full life cycle for our objects!

12.4 Inheritance: Letting Objects Share and Reuse Code

Now, let's make our code even more powerful by letting objects inherit from other objects! With inheritance, one class can take on the attributes and methods of another class, which means reusing code and building on existing functionality. It's like inheriting some awesome features from your parents!

Example:

```python
class Animal:
    def speak(self):
        print("Animal makes a sound")

class Dog(Animal):
    def speak(self):  # Overriding the method
        print("Woof!")

# Creating an object of Dog class
my_dog = Dog()
my_dog.speak()  # Output: Woof!
```

In this example, Dog inherits from Animal, but we've customized its behavior by overriding the speak() method. Inheritance allows for powerful reuse of code, and it just makes your life easier!

162

12.5 Encapsulation: Keeping Things Safe and Secure

Now, let's talk about encapsulation, which is all about keeping our objects safe and tidy. Encapsulation allows us to bundle data (attributes) and methods together and hide certain parts of the object from the outside world. This way, we control how the data is accessed and modified.

Example:

```python
class BankAccount:
    def __init__(self, balance):
        self.__balance = balance  # Private attribute

    def deposit(self, amount):
        if amount > 0:
            self.__balance += amount
        else:
            print("Deposit amount must be positive!")

    def get_balance(self):
        return self.__balance

# Creating an object
account = BankAccount(1000)
account.deposit(500)
print(account.get_balance())  # Output: 1500
```

Notice how the __balance attribute is private? It's hidden from the outside world, and we can only modify it through the methods we provide. This keeps the data safe from accidental changes and errors!

12.6 Polymorphism: The Magic of Multiple Forms

Let's wrap it up with polymorphism—a superpower that lets different objects respond to the same method in their own way. It's like a shape-shifter: one method, but different outcomes based on the object it's called on.

Example:

```python
class Cat:
    def speak(self):
        print("Meow!")

class Dog:
    def speak(self):
        print("Woof!")

# Using polymorphism
def animal_speak(animal):
    animal.speak()
```

```
dog = Dog()
cat = Cat()

animal_speak(dog)  # Output: Woof!
animal_speak(cat)  # Output: Meow!
```

Here, the speak() method is the same, but each object (dog and cat) does its own thing. This flexibility is the beauty of polymorphism.

Summary: You've Got This!

Look at you—coming up strong with Object-Oriented Programming! You've learned how to create classes and objects, add attributes and methods, and use inheritance, encapsulation, and polymorphism to write cleaner, more efficient code. OOP is a game-changer, and you're now ready to start organizing your code like a pro!

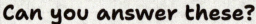

Can you answer these?

What is the main purpose of using classes in Object-Oriented Programming?

a) To store variables
b) To organize data and functions into reusable blueprints
c) To handle errors
d) To make programs run faster

Which of the following is the correct syntax to define a constructor in Python?

a) def init(self):
b) def __constructor__(self):
c) def __init__(self):
d) def initialize(self):

Find all the answers for the quiz in the answer key provided at the end!

Exercise 1: Class and Objects

Create a class called Car with the following attributes:

- make
- model
- year

Create a method called display_info()
that prints out the car's make, model,
and year. Then, create an object of the
Car class and call display_info() on it.

For exercise
solutions, check
out our support
at Github!

167

Exercise 2: Constructor and Destructor

Create a class called Book with the attributes title and author. Include a constructor to initialize these attributes and a destructor that prints "The book is being destroyed!" when the object is deleted. Create a book object and delete it to see the destructor in action.

Exercise 3: Inheritance

Create a base class called Person with attributes name and age, and a method introduce(). Then, create a subclass called Employee that inherits from Person and adds an attribute position. Override the introduce() method in the Employee class to print a personalized introduction with their name, age, and position. Create an employee object and call introduce() on it

Exercise 4: Encapsulation

Create a class called EmployeeAccount with a private attribute salary. Implement a method update_salary() that allows you to safely update the salary value. Include a method get_salary() that returns the current salary. Create an object of the class, update the salary, and print the updated salary.

Exercise 5: Polymorphism

Create two classes, Rectangle and Circle, both with a method area(). The Rectangle class should calculate the area as length * width, and the Circle class should calculate the area as π * radius^2. Create a function print_area() that accepts any shape object and prints its area. Demonstrate polymorphism by creating a Rectangle and a Circle object and passing them to print_area().

Next Up: Get ready to supercharge your projects! Next, we'll dive into working with libraries to expand your toolkit and amp up your coding abilities!

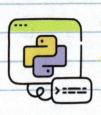

Working with Libraries & Packages

What are we going to learn?

1. Installing External Libraries with pip
2. Commonly Used Python Libraries: math, random, datetime
3. Introduction to numpy for Arrays and Data Analysis

Ever wondered what's faster and smarter? Writing all the code yourself, or using code that's already been written and optimized by someone else? If you're thinking the second option sounds more appealing, then libraries are the answer! Libraries save us time by providing pre-written code that we can simply import and use. It's like borrowing someone else's hard work to make your life easier—how cool is that?

In this section, we'll dive into the world of libraries and how to install, use, and work with them in Python!

170

13.1 Installing External Libraries with pip and pip3

So, Why **pip** and **pip3?**

You might have seen both pip and pip3 used when installing packages, and you might be wondering which one to use.

Here's the lowdown:

pip is the standard package manager for Python. You use it to install external libraries, but it's mainly associated with Python 2 (which is no longer supported).

pip3 is specifically for Python 3. If you have both Python 2 and Python 3 installed on your system, pip3 ensures you're installing packages for Python 3.

If you're working in a Python 3 environment, you'll mostly use pip3 to install libraries. If you're on a system where Python 3 is the only version installed, both pip and pip3 might work the same way. But just to be safe, use pip3!

How to install a library using pip:

```
pip install library_name
```
Terminal

For example, if you wanted to install a library called **requests** (great for working with web APIs), just type:

Let's say you want to install the popular **requests** library (used for making HTTP requests). You can do it with just one line of code:

```
pip3 install requests   # For Python 3
```
Terminal

Or, if your system defaults to Python 3, you might be able to use just:

```
pip install requests   # This works for Python 3 on some systems too
```
Terminal

Pro Tip

You can install multiple libraries at once by separating them with spaces! Here's an example:

```
pip install numpy pandas matplotlib
```
`Terminal`

Boom! All three libraries installed at once.

Fun Fact:

There are over 300,000 libraries available on the Python Package Index (PyPI). The possibilities are endless!

13.2 Commonly Used Python Libraries: math, random, datetime

Before we dive into the heavy-duty libraries, let's talk about some built-in libraries that come with Python—these don't need to be installed, and they're packed with useful functions!

math: Need to do some quick math? The math library has built-in functions for advanced math operations like square roots and trigonometric functions.

Example:

```
import math
print(math.sqrt(16))  # Output: 4.0
```

Using math functions is often faster than writing your own complex math calculations. So next time you need a quick formula, check out math!

random: Want to add a little unpredictability to your program? The random library helps you generate random numbers, shuffle lists, or pick random items!

FUN FACT

Randomness is used in everything from gaming to cryptography. So when you need something unpredictable, just let random do the work!

Example:

```
import random
print(random.randint(1, 10)) # Output: Random
number between 1 and 10
```

datetime: Working with dates and times? The datetime library is perfect for managing dates, times, and intervals!

TOP TIPS

Want to track the current date and time in your program? datetime makes it easy to handle time zones and specific time intervals—no need for manual calculations!

Example:

```
import datetime
current_time = datetime.datetime.now()
print(current_time) # Output: Current date and time
```

13.3 Introduction to NumPy for Arrays and Data Analysis

Now, let's level up a bit! If you want to work with large datasets or perform quick mathematical operations on arrays, NumPy is your go-to library. It's one of the most popular libraries for data analysis, and it lets you handle arrays—think of them like lists, but way faster and more powerful!

How to install NumPy:

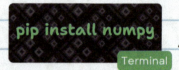

```
pip install numpy
```
Terminal

Quick Example:

Creating an array with NumPy and performing a calculation:

```python
import numpy as np

# Create an array
arr = np.array([1, 2, 3, 4, 5])

# Add 2 to each element in the array
arr = arr + 2
print(arr)  # Output: [3 4 5 6 7]
```

Pro Tip: NumPy allows you to perform vectorized operations, which means you can apply a calculation to an entire array at once! This is much faster than using loops.

Fun Fact:

NumPy is the useful with many other popular libraries, like Pandas (for data manipulation) and Matplotlib (for data visualization), so mastering NumPy will set you up for success in data science and analytics!

Summary:
You've just unlocked the secret to working smarter, not harder. By using libraries and packages, you're tapping into a wealth of pre-written code that's ready to make your life easier. Whether it's performing calculations with math, adding randomness with random, handling dates with datetime, or analyzing data with NumPy, libraries allow you to do more in less time.

Can you answer these?

Which of the following is a built-in Python library that allows you to work with dates and times?

a) random
b) math
c) datetime
d) requests

What does the math.sqrt() function do?

a) Computes the square of a number
b) Computes the square root of a number
c) Computes the sum of squares of two numbers
d) Computes the factorial of a number

What does the following code print?

```
import random
print(random.randint(1, 10))
```

a) A random integer between 1 and 10
b) A random float between 1 and 10
c) A random string between 1 and 10
d) A random boolean value

Find all the answers for the quiz in the answer key provided at the end!

178

Quick Exercise

Exercise 1: Installing and Using a Library

- Install the requests library using pip3 (or pip if you're using Python 3 by default).
- Write a program that uses the requests library to make a GET request to a public API (like https://jsonplaceholder.typicode.com/posts) and print the first post's title.

Exercise 2: Randomness and DateTime

- Write a Python program that:
  - Generates a random number between 1 and 100 using the random library.
  - Prints the current date and time using the datetime library.

For exercise solutions, check out our support at Github!

Exercise 3: NumPy Arrays

- Create a NumPy array of the following numbers: [5, 10, 15, 20, 25].
- Use NumPy to:
  - Add 10 to each element in the array.
  - Multiply each element by 2.
  - Print the modified array.

Exercise 4: Math Operations

- Import the math library.
- Write a program that:
  - Takes a number as input from the user.
  - Prints the square root, sine, and cosine of that number (use math.sqrt(), math.sin(), and math.cos()).

Next Up:

Hold on tight, buddy! It's time for the moment you've been waiting for—building your very own Python application! We'll build it step-by-step, test, debug, and polish the code. Ready to bring your skills to life? Let's go!!

Project:

Building a Small Python Application

What are we going to learn?

1. Defining the Project Scope
2. Building the Application Step-by-Step
3. Testing and Debugging
4. Documenting the Code
5. Everything in Action

Yes, We've come a long way already, haven't we? All the concepts, all the lines of code, the libraries—now it's time to put everything into practice. Ready to bring your skills to life?

In this chapter, we're going to **build a small Python application.** The cool part is, you'll be able to look back and say, "I did that!"

But before we jump into building, let's break it down and **plan our steps carefully.** 181

14.1 Defining the Project Scope

Okay, before we go all-in, let's take a step back and **define the project.** This is critical because jumping into code without a clear plan is like going on a road trip without a map—you'll definitely get lost!

Here's what you need to do:

Understand what the project is about: What's the application supposed to do? What problem does it solve?

Identify the core features: Start with the basics and add more features as you go. Don't try to build a huge app in one go. Rome wasn't built in a day, right?

Set a clear goal: Know what your final product should look like so you don't get sidetracked along the way.

14.2 Building the Application Step-by-Step

Now, it's time to get our hands dirty! This is where we take all that knowledge we've learned and start coding.

But remember—small steps are the way to go:

Start simple: Set up the project structure, create files, and make sure everything is ready.

Break the project into parts: Don't try to build everything at once. Work on one feature at a time and keep testing along the way.

Write clean, readable code: This is your future self talking to you. You'll thank yourself later when you look back at your code and it makes sense!

For example, if you're building a simple to-do list app, you can start with just:

- A list to store tasks.
- Code to add a task.
- Code to remove a task.

14.3 Testing and Debugging

I know, I know—**testing and debugging** may sound a little scary, but it's one of the most important parts of coding!

It's like taking a test—no one likes it, but it's necessary to pass!

Here's the thing: **code doesn't always work the first time,** and that's totally okay. The key is to be patient, test your code in **small chunks**, and use tools like **print statements** or even Python's built-in **debugger** to track down those bugs.

Test often: Don't wait until the end to test everything. Test each feature as you go!

Debugging: If something's not working, read the error messages carefully, and work through the problem step-by-step.

Fun Fact: Did you know that even the best programmers get errors? It's all part of the process! So don't stress— you'll get there!

14.4 Documenting the Code

Now, let's talk about something super important: documenting your code. It may seem like extra work, but trust me, you'll thank yourself later. Documentation makes your code readable and helps others understand your project.

Here's how you can do it:

Write clear comments: Explain what each section of code does. You don't need to write a novel, just enough to make it easy to follow.

Use docstrings: For functions and classes, docstrings help others (and future you) understand what the function does and how to use it.

Keep things tidy: A well-documented project is way easier to maintain and share.

185

14.5 Everything in Action

We'll build a simple To-Do List App, and by the end of this, you'll have a fully functional project. Ready? Let's dive in!

Project: Build a Simple To-Do List Application

Our goal is to create a command-line To-Do List application. The app will let the user:

- Add tasks to a list.
- View all tasks.
- Mark tasks as complete.
- Delete tasks.

This project will help us practice functions, loops, and file handling.

Step 1: Defining the Project Scope

Before we get into the code, let's plan what our app will do:

- **Add Task:** The user can input a new task and it will be added to the list.
- **View Tasks:** The user can view all the tasks they've entered.
- **Mark Task as Complete:** The user can mark a task as done.
- **Delete Task:** The user can delete a task from the list.
- **Save Tasks:** We'll store tasks in a file so they persist even when the program is closed.

186

Step 2: Set Up Your Project

Create a folder for your project called todo_app. Inside it, create a Python file called todo.py and a text file called tasks.txt where we will save our tasks.

Your folder structure should look like this:

todo_app/
    todo.py
    tasks.txt

Step 3: Write the Code

Let's start coding the application!
We'll break it down step-by-step.

1. Opening and Reading the Task File
Let's start by loading the existing tasks from the tasks.txt file when the app starts.

```python
pdef load_tasks():
    try:
        with open("tasks.txt", "r") as file:
            tasks = file.readlines()
            tasks = [task.strip() for task in tasks]  # Clean up newlines
    except FileNotFoundError:
        tasks = []  # If file doesn't exist, return an empty list
    return tasks
```

This function will:
- Try to open tasks.txt.
- If the file exists, it will read the tasks and strip any extra newlines.
- If the file doesn't exist (first run), it will return an empty list.

2. Saving the Tasks
Next, we need a function to save the tasks back to the file after every change.

```
def save_tasks(tasks):
    with open("tasks.txt", "w") as file:
        for task in tasks:
            file.write(f"{task}\n")
```

This function will:
- Open the tasks.txt file in write mode.
- Write each task to the file, each on a new line.

3. Add a Task
Now let's allow the user to add a new task.

```
def add_task(tasks):
    task = input("Enter a new task: ")
    tasks.append(task)  # Add the task to the list
    print(f"Task '{task}' added!")
    save_tasks(tasks)
```

This function will:
- Prompt the user to enter a new task.
- Add it to the list of tasks.
- Save the updated list of tasks to the file.

4. View All Tasks
Let's create a function to view all tasks:

```
def view_tasks(tasks):
    if not tasks:
        print("No tasks available!")
    else:
        print("Your tasks:")
        for i, task in enumerate(tasks, 1):
            print(f"{i}. {task}")
```

This function will:
- Check if there are any tasks.
- If there are, it will print each task with a number beside it.

5. Mark Task as Complete

Now, we need a function that allows the user to mark a task as complete. Let's just append "(Completed)" to the task.

```python
def mark_task_complete(tasks):
    view_tasks(tasks)  # First, show the tasks
    try:
        task_number = int(input("Enter the task number to mark as complete: "))
        task = tasks[task_number - 1]
        tasks[task_number - 1] = task + " (Completed)"
        print(f"Task '{task}' marked as complete!")
        save_tasks(tasks)
    except (ValueError, IndexError):
        print("Invalid task number.")
```

This function will:
- Show the list of tasks.
- Ask the user to enter the number of the task to mark as complete.
- Update the task with the text " (Completed)" and save the tasks.

6. Delete Task
Finally, let's add the ability to delete a task.

```python
def delete_task(tasks):
    view_tasks(tasks)  # Show all tasks
    try:
        task_number = int(input("Enter the task number to delete: "))
        task = tasks.pop(task_number - 1)
        print(f"Task '{task}' deleted!")
        save_tasks(tasks)
    except (ValueError, IndexError):
        print("Invalid task number.")
```

This function will:
- Show the list of tasks.
- Allow the user to delete a task by selecting its number.
- Remove the task from the list and save the updated list.

7. Main Menu
Now, let's put everything together with a main menu so the user can choose what to do:

```python
def main():
    tasks = load_tasks()  # Load tasks when the app starts
```

```
while True:
    print("\nTo-Do List Application")
    print("1. Add Task")
    print("2. View Tasks")
    print("3. Mark Task as Complete")
    print("4. Delete Task")
    print("5. Exit")

    choice = input("Choose an option: ")

    if choice == "1":
        add_task(tasks)
    elif choice == "2":
        view_tasks(tasks)
    elif choice == "3":
        mark_task_complete(tasks)
    elif choice == "4":
        delete_task(tasks)
    elif choice == "5":
        print("Goodbye!")
        break
    else:
        print("Invalid option. Please try again.")

if __name__ == "__main__":
    main()
```

Step 4: Running the Project

Now that you have the code, it's time to run the app!
When you run todo.py, the app will:

- Show the main menu.
- Let you add, view, mark complete, or delete tasks.
- Save your tasks to the file tasks.txt so they persist
  even when you exit the program.

192

Step 5: Testing and Debugging

Test each part of the application:

- Try adding multiple tasks and check if they appear in the task list.
- Mark a task as complete and make sure it updates correctly.
- Try deleting tasks and ensure they are removed from both the list and the file.

Don't forget—debugging is part of the process. If something breaks, carefully read the error message and fix it step-by-step. You're doing great!

Step 6: Documenting the Code

Here's an example of how we can add comments to make our code more readable for future reference.

```python
def add_task(tasks):
    """
    Adds a new task to the task list and saves it to the file.
    """
    task = input("Enter a new task: ")
    tasks.append(task)  # Add the task to the list
    print(f"Task '{task}' added!")
    save_tasks(tasks)  # Save tasks to file
```

193

By documenting your code, you ensure that others (and future you) can understand how everything works!

Pro Tip: If you ever plan to share your code or work with a team, good documentation is a must! It makes collaboration way smoother. 💡

Fun Fact: Did you know that some of the best open-source projects in the world, like TensorFlow and Flask, are well-documented? Good documentation is one of the keys to making your project successful and useful to others!

Summary:

You've done an amazing job so far! You've learned all the tools and techniques, and now it's time to bring it all together into a real project. Here's what you've done in this chapter:

- Defined the scope of your project and set clear goals.
- Built your application step-by-step with clean code and small features.
- Tested and debugged your code to make sure everything runs smoothly.
- Documented your code so it's easy to understand, even months from now.

Practice! Practice and Practice !!

Build these 5 projects yourself to practice the concepts.

You can find the code for these projects on our GitHub page

1. Age Calculator

Objective: Calculate a person's age based on their birth year.

Key Concepts: Date and time operations, user input.

Hint:

* Use the datetime module to get the current year.
* Take the user's birth year as input.
* Calculate and display their age.

2. Simple Calculator

Objective: A basic calculator that performs addition, subtraction, multiplication, and division.

Key Concepts: Functions, user input, math operators.

> **Hint:**
> * Create functions for each operation.
> * Take user input for the operation and numbers.
> * Display the result.

3. Simple Quiz

Objective: A basic quiz program with multiple-choice questions.

Key Concepts: Dictionaries, loops, and conditionals.

Hint:
* Store questions and answers in a dictionary.
* Loop through the questions and compare user input with the correct answers.
* Keep track of the score.

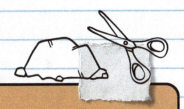

4. Rock, Paper, Scissors Game

Objective: A simple game where the user plays against the computer.

Key Concepts: Random numbers, conditional statements, and loops.

Hint:
* Use random.choice() to select the computer's move.
* Take user input for their move.
* Compare moves to decide the winner.

5. Password Generator

Objective: Generate a random password with letters, numbers, and symbols.

Key Concepts: Strings, loops, and the random module.

Hint:
* Create lists of letters, numbers, and symbols.
* Use random.choice() to pick characters.
* Combine them to form a password.

Next Steps in Python

What are we going to learn?

1. Exploring Advanced Topics in Python
2. Resources for Further Learning
3. Overview of Specialized Areas (e.g., Web Development, Data Science)

Hey, superstar! ☀️ You've come a long way, and now it's time to take those Python skills of yours to new heights. But guess what? The world of Python is HUGE, and there are so many exciting areas you can explore next! 💡

Let's talk about advanced topics in Python. These will help you level up and tackle complex problems like a pro. Whether it's Machine Learning, Web Development, or Data Science, there's always something new to master. With Python, the possibilities are endless!

15.1 Exploring Advanced Topics in Python

The real magic happens when you dive into the more advanced topics. Want to build cool web apps? Check out Flask or Django. Interested in crunching numbers or analyzing data? You've got libraries like Pandas, NumPy, and Matplotlib waiting for you. And if you're curious about AI and Machine Learning, you've got TensorFlow, Keras, and PyTorch to explore!

The deeper you go, the more powerful your Python skills will become. But don't worry, we'll make sure you have all the resources and guidance you need to keep learning at your own pace.

15.2 Resources for Further Learning

Here's the exciting part: there are tons of resources out there to help you continue your Python journey. Whether it's books, online courses, forums, or tutorials—everything you need is just a click away.

199

Books: "Automate the Boring Stuff with Python" and "Python Crash Course" are two great reads that dive deeper into Python. If you have liked this book, which i am hoping since you have come this far, then you must check out our other books as well for more in-depth knowledge!

Websites and Communities: Check out Python.org, Stack Overflow, Join Our Community for more personalised learning and growth!

Online Courses: Websites like Udemy, Coursera, and edX offer detailed Python courses for every level. You can also find tons of Python tutorials on YouTube. Be sure to check out our YouTube Channel and Udemy Page for step-by-step guides!

You can stay connected with us on our other social platforms using the handles below:

- Instagram
- Youtube
- Linkedin
- Website
- Community - Skool

You will find detailed coding resources for this book, along with many other books and courses, at our GitHub

Pro Tip: Don't be afraid to ask questions or join our Python community! We are always willing to help.

Overview of Specialized Areas

Web Development

Want to build websites and web applications? Python is awesome for that. Frameworks like Django and Flask allow you to create powerful, scalable web apps without much hassle. Imagine building your own social media platform or an e-commerce site!

Data Science

Python is the go-to language for data analysis and visualization. With libraries like Pandas, NumPy, and Matplotlib, you can analyze massive datasets, uncover insights, and even build predictive models. Data Science is booming right now, and Python is at the heart of it.

Machine Learning and AI

This is where things get really exciting. With libraries like TensorFlow and Scikit-learn, you can start building your own machine learning models, train them, and even deploy them for real-world use cases. From recommendation systems to self-driving cars, Python is making it all possible!

Automation

Want to automate those boring, repetitive tasks? Python can handle that too. With just a few lines of code, you can automate emails, file management, data collection, and much more. It's like giving your computer a mind of its own!

201

Final Thoughts

I hope you are feeling content! But the journey doesn't stop here, my friend. Python is an endless adventure, and every step you take opens up new and exciting opportunities. Whether you decide to go deep into web development, explore the world of data science, or dive into AI and machine learning, Python will be your best friend!

If you have some this far!

 Follow our Linkedin Page

 Follow us on Medium Blog

 Join our learning community on Skool
"Break into IT with Python"

☑ Check out the code files, project
Solutions and exercise solutions on Github

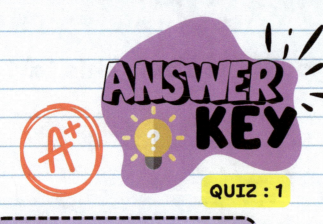

ANSWER KEY

A+

Q1: What is one advantage of programming a task for a machine?

Correct Answer: c) Machines efficiently handle repetitive and complex tasks.

Programming tasks for machines allows for automation, which significantly enhances efficiency in performing repetitive and complex tasks without human intervention.

Fill in the blank:

1. Natural languages
2. Assembly language

Q1: How can you verify if Python was installed correctly?

Correct Answer: c) Type python --version in the command line

This command displays the installed Python version and confirms that Python is correctly installed.

Q2: What command do you use to create a virtual environment named myenv?

Correct Answer: c) python -m venv myenv

This is the correct syntax for creating a virtual environment named myenv.

204

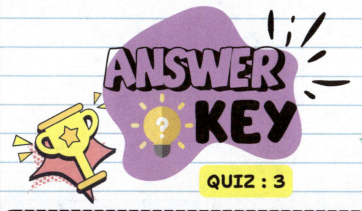

ANSWER KEY

QUIZ : 3

Q1: In the following code, which line(s) are correctly indented for the function to work properly?

Correct Answer: c) The print line needs to be indented under def

In Python, code within a function must be indented. The print line should be indented to indicate it belongs to the greet() function. Correctly indented code would look like this:

python
Copy code

```
def greet():
    print("Hello, World!")
```

Q2: What is the purpose of a docstring in a Python function?

Correct Answer: b) To document what the function does for future reference

A docstring is a string literal used to describe the purpose and functionality of a function, making the code more understandable for others (or for yourself later). Example:

python
Copy code

```
def greet():
    """This function prints a greeting message."""
    print("Hello, World!")
```

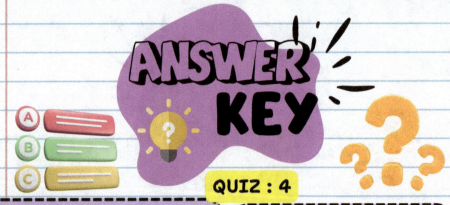

QUIZ : 4

Q1:l Which of the following is a convention in Python for declaring a constant?

Correct Answer: c) Using uppercase letters, like PI.

In Python, constants are typically declared using uppercase letters to indicate that they should not be changed, following the naming convention of PEP 8

Q2: What type of data is stored in the variable price = 19.99?

Correct Answer: b) Float.

The value 19.99 is a decimal number, which is classified as a float in Python

Q3: Which of these would correctly store a Boolean value?

Correct Answer: c) is_open = True.

In Python, Boolean values are represented by the keywords True and False, and they must be capitalized

Q4: If age = "30" is a string, which of the following would convert age to an integer?

Correct Answer: c) int(age).

The int() function is used to convert a string that represents a number into an integer in Python

ANSWER KEY

Q1: What will this code print?
python

```python
x = 10
y = 20
print(x > 5 and y < 25)
```

Correct Answer: a) True.

The expression x > 5 evaluates to True and y < 25 also evaluates to True. Since both conditions are true, the and operator returns True

Q2: Which of the following statements is correct about the += operator?

Correct Answer: b) x += y is the same as x = x + y.

The += operator adds the right operand to the left operand and assigns the result to the left operand, effectively making it equivalent to x = x + y

Q1: What will this code output?

```
for i in range(5):
    if i == 3:
        pass
    else:
        print(i)
```

Correct Answer: a) 0 1 2 4.

The loop iterates over the range of 5 (0 to 4). When ii equals 3, the pass statement is executed, which does nothing and allows the loop to continue. Therefore, the values 0, 1, 2, and 4 are printed.

Q2: Which of the following keywords would you use if you want to skip the current iteration and continue with the next iteration?

Correct Answer: b) continue.

The continue statement is specifically used in Python to skip the remainder of the current loop iteration and proceed to the next iteration. In contrast, pass does nothing, break exits the loop entirely, and return is used to exit a function.

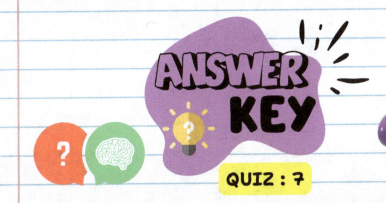

Q1: What does a function return if there is no return statement?

Correct Answer: c) None.

In Python, if a function does not have a return statement, it implicitly returns None when called .

Q2: Which scope is only accessible inside the function where it's declared?

Correct Answer: a) Local scope.

A variable created inside a function belongs to the local scope of that function and can only be accessed within that function .

Q3: Which of the following is a built-in function in Python?

Correct Answer: c) print().

The print() function is a built-in function in Python used to output data to the console, while the other options are not standard built-in functions .

QUIZ : 8

Q1: Which of the following methods adds an item to the end of a list?

Correct Answer: b) append().

The append() method is specifically designed to add an item to the end of a list in Python, modifying the list in place

Q3: Which of the following statements is true about dictionaries?

Correct Answer: c) Dictionaries store data in key-value pairs.

This statement accurately describes dictionaries in Python, which are collections of key-value pairs, while the other options contain inaccuracies regarding their properties

Q2: What will the following code output?

```
data = {"city": "Paris", "population": 2000000}
data["country"] = "France"
print(data)
```

Correct Answer: b) {"city": "Paris", "population": 2000000, "country": "France"}.

The code adds a new key-value pair for "country" to the existing dictionary, resulting in the output that includes all three key-value pairs

QUIZ : 9

Q1: What will the following code output?

```
name = "Alice"
age = 30
print(f"Name: {name}, Age: {age}")
```

Correct Answer: a) Name: Alice, Age: 30.

The code uses an f-string to format the output, which correctly substitutes the values of name and age into the string, resulting in "Name: Alice, Age: 30" being printed .

Q2: What will the following code output?

```
word = "Python"
print(word * 3)
```

Correct Answer: a) PythonPythonPython.

The multiplication operator * is used to repeat the string "Python" three times, producing "PythonPythonPython" as the output .

ANSWER KEY

Q1: What will the following code output?

```
try:
    num = int("not_a_number")
except ValueError:
    print("Invalid number!")
else:
    print("Conversion successful!")
finally:
    print("End of program.")
```

Correct Answer: a) Invalid number!

End of program.
The code attempts to convert a string that cannot be converted to an integer, which raises a ValueError. The exception is caught in the except block, printing "Invalid number!". The finally block then executes, printing "End of program.".

Q2: What will the following code output?

```python
def check_age(age):
    if age < 0:
        raise ValueError("Age can't be negative!")
    else:
        print("Age is valid.")

try:
    check_age(-5)
except ValueError as e:
    print(e)
```

Correct Answer: c) Age can't be negative!
function check_age raises a ValueError when a
negative age is passed. This exception is caught
in the except block, which prints the error
message "Age can't be negative!".

ANSWER KEY

Q1: What does the following code do?

```
with open("data.txt", "w") as file:
    file.write("Hello, Python!")
```

Correct Answer: b)

Writes "Hello, Python!" to data.txt and creates it if it doesn't exist.
The code opens (or creates if it doesn't exist) a file named "data.txt" in write mode ("w") and writes the string "Hello, Python!" into it. If the file already exists, its content will be overwritten

Q2: In a try-except block for file handling, what will this code output if the file doesn't exist?

```
try:
    with open("missing.txt", "r") as file:
        data = file.read()
except FileNotFoundError:
    print("File not found!")
```

Correct Answer: b) File not found!

Since "missing.txt" does not exist, a FileNotFoundError is raised, which is caught by the except block, resulting in the output "File not found!"

ANSWER KEY

Q1: What is the main purpose of using classes in Object-Oriented Programming?

Correct Answer: b) To organize data and functions into reusable blueprints.

Classes serve as blueprints for creating objects, encapsulating data and methods that operate on that data, which promotes code reusability and organization in software development

Q2: Which of the following is the correct syntax to define a constructor in Python?

Correct Answer: c) def init(self):

In Python, the constructor is defined using the __init__ method, which is automatically called when a new object of the class is created

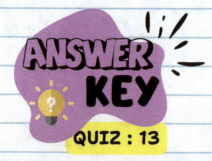

Q1: Which of the following is a built-in Python library that allows you to work with dates and times?

Correct Answer: c) datetime.

The datetime module in Python provides classes for manipulating dates and times, making it the appropriate choice for working with date and time data .

Q2: What does the math.sqrt() function do?

Correct Answer: b) Computes the square root of a number.

The math.sqrt() function is used to calculate the square root of a given non-negative number, returning the result as a floating-point value .

Q3: What does the following code print?

```
import random
print(random.randint(1, 10))
```

Correct Answer: a) A random integer between 1 and 10.

The random.randint(1, 10) function generates and returns a random integer within the inclusive range from 1 to 10 .

216

Start your Python journey the most engaging way!

The book takes up the very basics of python and present to the reader - a visually simplified explanation, that is easy & quick to understand.

It will keep you Engaged until the very last page!

Difficult concepts made easy through :

Illustrative Examples Visual Explanations

 Online Support

Educational doodles Practice exercise and projects

COMING SOON

Vol 1.2
Built-in Data Structures in Python

Vol 1.3
Python Scripting and Automation

Vol 1.4
Object-Oriented Programming (OOP) & Design in Python

Join us on Skool
https://www.skool.com/
pythonlearningcommunity

www.ingramcontent.com/pod-product-compliance
Lightning Source LLC
LaVergne TN
LVHW051733050326
832903LV00023B/903